YOUR FAITH HUNT

A 21-day Devotional and Prayer Journal

GARY KEESEE

ISBN: 978-1-945930-36-2

Printed by Free Indeed Publishers.
Distributed by Faith Life Now.

Faith Life Now
P.O. Box 779
New Albany, OH 43054
1-(888)-391-LIFE

You can reach Faith Life Now Ministries on the Internet at www.faithlifenow.com

To Drenda, who put up with my hunting
for all of these years.

CONTENTS

INTRODUCTION

Hunt /hənt/ 1. *search determinedly for someone or something; search for something until it is found; to pursue and capture.*

Could I possibly believe what I was seeing? The deer seemed to be coming in the order that I had sowed for them.

The stories for *Faith Hunt*, the original book, started while I lived in Oklahoma. At the time, Oklahoma had a one-deer limit. Later when I moved to Ohio, Ohio had a three-deer limit, but only one could be a buck. The other two had to be does or what is called a button buck. A button buck is a young buck with antlers less than three inches in length. Since they're so small, it's hard to see them at all, and the buck can easily be mistaken for a doe. To avoid confusion, the state of Ohio made button bucks count as does in the yearly bag limit.

So when I moved to Ohio, I would sow my seed for a buck and either a button buck or a doe. In the preceding two years before this story happened, I had sown for a buck and a doe and had successfully harvested *both* the buck and the doe in those years, usually within 40 minutes of being in the field.

But this particular year, I had a strange thought: *The deer were coming in the order that I wrote them down on my seed.* (I usually wrote on my check when I sowed, "for a buck four-point or bigger and one doe.") The buck would come first, and then the doe would show up. Were they coming in the order I had written them on my seed check? Could it be possible?

It seemed incredible to consider, so I decided to test my theory and this time reverse the order in which I sowed my seed. I wrote "for a doe and a buck" on my seed instead of for a buck and a doe. Sure enough, the doe came first that year followed by the buck.

I was shocked! Again, I decided to test my observations with another experiment. I told my son Tim what I was doing and what God was showing me.

That year, I sowed for a seven-point buck. I decided that an eight-point would be too normal, as deer typically have four-points on each side. A seven-point, although not *that* uncommon in itself, was a very specific harvest, one which I believed would prove my theory.

So, Drenda and I sowed our seed that year for a seven-point buck and believed that we received when we prayed.

As the season opened at the beginning of October, I was surprised by the fact that I felt no desire to go out. In fact, all through October, I had no desire to go out. The woods had come alive with the colors of fall, and I usually really enjoyed going out this time of year, but something was different.

When November came and I still felt this way, I grew concerned. What was going on?

Then it happened. Drenda's parents were in town visiting from Alabama and were leaving the next morning. That night, the night before they would be leaving, all of a sudden, I KNEW I had to go out the next morning. It was hard to explain, but I just knew I had to go out! I told everyone that I was going out in the morning to get my deer.

The next morning, I got up before sunrise. The temperature was cool, but it was going to be a sunny day. I put on my light camo coveralls, grabbed my grunt call and my Horton Legend crossbow, and headed to my stand. At the time, Drenda and I owned 55 acres of land, with about 30 acres of that being woods and marsh. Over the previous years, I had hunted in the woods and did great, but this year I decided to put up a stand along the marsh in the brushy area of the property. There were some great trails there, and scrapes were common as well. I felt sure the new stand would produce deer.

Unfortunately, because this new stand was in such a brushy area, it really didn't offer great visibility. I could really only see about 40 yards in any direction, and to have a good shot, the deer needed to basically come under my tree. So I placed the stand directly above the intersection of two deer trails that ran along the marsh, thinking that if the deer moved along those two trails, I would be ready for them.

With the early morning dawn approaching, I walked the 300 yards and made my way up to the metal stand, which sat 21 feet off the ground. The morning slowly came alive with the usual activity: a squirrel barking, birds chirping, crows calling to each other, and geese honking as they flew overhead. It was a beautiful morning, and everything was perfect with one exception: I didn't see any deer.

The sun had been up for about 30 minutes and I hadn't seen one deer, but I knew the area was a bedding area and the deer would be moving into it later in the morning. But I had a problem. *Drenda's parents were leaving*. In fact, I could hear them loading the car up at the house, and I wanted to say good-bye to them before they left.

Reluctantly, I got down out of the stand and started for the house. I knew I felt the Holy Spirit tell me that today was the day and that the new marsh stand was the place to be for my seven-pointer. As I made my way to the house, I understood that it wasn't God's fault that I was walking to the house without a deer. I knew they came to the marsh later in the morning, and I just didn't have time to wait for them. I figured I would just have to go out again at a later date to bag the seven-pointer.

As I arrived at the house, Drenda informed me that none of them had eaten breakfast yet and asked if I would cook my famous waffles and eggs for her parents. I said, "Of course," and began to scramble some eggs.

Before I was half finished, something caught my eye outside our kitchen window that looks out over our marsh and woods. A couple of does were trotting across the back of the property. As I looked closer, I spotted a buck trailing them. They were headed toward the marsh, and I knew they would be going directly under my stand on their way there. I also knew that if I hurried, I felt I could beat them there and be in my stand when they arrived—if I hurried!

I shouted for someone to take over cooking and said, "There's my buck! I'll be back in a minute!"

I quickly ran out the door, grabbed my Horton, and headed to the stand. The path the deer were on took them through the brush, and I knew they wouldn't see me as I came in the opposite side of the marsh. The only problem was speed. Could I beat them there?

I got to the tree and was glad I hadn't seen them yet. Out

of breath, I climbed up the tree and loaded a bolt onto the crossbow and sat down. Then I saw them. The does were coming down the path that I was sure they would be using. And, sure enough, the buck wasn't far behind. They were moving fairly quickly in a trot as they made their way toward the tree.

The does trotted past me, but the buck slowed to a walk as he approached the tree. He was only about 25 yards away from me walking broadside to me. I knew this was the moment, so I put the Legend's peep site on him and let the arrow fly. I knew the minute I fired that I had pulled it off.

With my heart racing from running to the tree then climbing it, my hands weren't really steady. I saw the arrow hit the buck low, somewhere around the low front shoulder. I was hoping that it had hit high enough to hit the lungs, but I couldn't tell since the buck took off into the brush.

I waited for about 20 minutes and got down to examine my arrow. There was blood on the arrow, but I couldn't tell how good of a hit it was. I knew the buck would stay in the brush and would bed down, so I decided to go back to the house, have some breakfast, and maybe come back out in three hours to track the buck.

Drenda and I said good-bye to her parents, and I explained to my sons what had happened and shared with them my plan to search our field for the buck. We decided that we would line up across our field and slowly move through the field. We were hoping the buck was dead, but if it jumped up, we were hoping one of us could get off a shot at it.

So we lined up across the brush-filled field and slowly started making our way across it. We had only gone about 30 yards when the buck jumped up. Apparently, Tim had jumped it up on the other side of the field. The buck was now leaping through the high brush moving away from Tim and directly toward Tom, who was in the middle of the field. Upon seeing Tom, the buck suddenly stopped, deciding which way to go. It hadn't seen me yet, so it stood broadside to me at about 60 or 70 yards, too far for my Horton.

But I knew this was my only chance. I guessed at how high I should aim the crossbow above the buck and let the arrow fly. I watched as the arrow made a slow arch toward the deer. In amazement, I saw it hit the deer directly in the middle of the neck. The arrow was now sticking through the neck with an equal amount of the arrow sticking out each side of the neck. The buck then bolted and was gone.

I watched carefully to determine the direction it took. I

had no idea if the neck shot would be a killing shot or not. I slowly made my way toward the spot I last saw the buck, moving very slowly so as to not spook it. I then spotted the buck lying down in a grassy spot with its head high about 50 yards from me. I decided to back out quietly and leave the buck alone. A few hours later, I went back to see if the buck was still where I had seen it earlier and it was not. But I spotted it about 20 yards further from where I had seen it earlier. It was still alive, but I now knew it was severely injured. I had to go to church for the evening but decided that Tim and I would come back out after church with flashlights to check on the buck.

Tim and I arrived home from church with excitement, hoping the buck was dead and eager to see if it was a seven-point. Up until that point, I really hadn't determined if it was indeed a seven-point or not. Tim and I made our way to the spot where I had last seen the buck, and it wasn't there. So we began to look around the area, and in a few minutes, I found the buck lying in some briars. He was dead.

Tim came over, and we drug it out of the briar patch and looked at the rack. It had four points on one side and three on the other. It was, in fact, a seven-point. Interestingly, as we studied the deer, we saw it was an eight-point with one tine broken off, which made it a seven-point! Wow, right?!

We praised God together as we stood in awe of the Kingdom.

At that moment, I realized why I didn't have an urge to go hunting in October—the buck I had sown for wasn't there yet!

You must know this before we really can talk about receiving from God.

Follow the unction of the Holy Spirit! There is no use in just going out in your own strength and sitting day after day waiting for what you've sown for to show up.

And the more specific your request, the more specific the timing!

The Kingdom of God is very specific, detailed actually! And knowing that the Kingdom of God works through laws—very specific laws—has changed my life.

It's been 16 years since I wrote *Faith Hunt*, the book I consider to be the recording of how God used something small in my life to help me discover the grandness of how His Kingdom operates—*to help me discover how faith works.*

If you've read *Faith Hunt*, you know my "faith hunt" applied to literal hunts. I love hunting, and God easily used my love for it to teach me His principles. *Faith Hunt* records many of those hunts up until 2001, when I shot the monster buck. (Since then, the stories have continued.)

God taught me many things about the Kingdom through deer hunting, starting with sowing a seed for my deer while claiming Mark 11:24: Therefore I tell you, whatever you ask for in prayer, believe that you have received it, and it will be yours.

Since that time, I've never failed to get my deer, usually within an hour, many times in just minutes. Never in the past 30 years has a deer come under my tree stand that was not the exact deer that I had sown for—*never*.

Our lives were completely changed by the things I learned in those days of small beginnings.

My life was changed radically by the power of God, and it's my life goal that people know that.

You may have heard my story before. Years before Drenda and I were in ministry, things just weren't working. I worked hard, but I just couldn't seem to make enough money to pay my bills, let alone get ahead. When I came up short each month, I would borrow to make ends meet, hoping to be able to pay it back the next month. But after a few years of living like that, I found myself in a financial pit, owing on 10 maxed-out credit cards, three finance company loans, two car payments, back taxes, judgments and liens, and $26,000 to relatives! I was drowning in debt and completely fed up.

And I had a family to provide for. All seven of us were living in a small, broken-down, 1800s farmhouse, complete with weeds growing through the broken window panes. Our cars were broken-down, too—with bent frames, rusted out floorboards, and mileage at more than 200,000 on each of them.

We lived like that for NINE very long years, and we were the Christians in our families!

There's much more to our story, but to keep it brief, we went from financial ruin to being completely debt free over the next two and a half years. We paid cash for cars and for our dream house. *Our lives drastically changed.*

Ever since then, I've been sharing my hunting stories and the Kingdom principles I learned from hunting. As Drenda and I began to teach what God taught us, we began to hear so many stories of how the Kingdom of God was changing other people's lives just like it did ours.

And, because Drenda and I love stories of how God has changed lives, we share *our* own story as often as possible, as well as the stories of others who have come to understand how the Kingdom works and have seen incredible things happen in their own lives as a result.

We've packed this book with plenty of those stories.

Of course, every person's "faith hunt" is unique to them, and your "faith hunt" may not look at all like mine, or like the ones you read in this book. You may not even be a hunter in the literal sense of the word.

But whether you're a hunter or not, I hope that these stories of the power and principles of the Kingdom of God each impact your life in some way, and that you're not just enthralled by the exciting stories in both this book and in *Faith Hunt* but motivated to believe God for more than you can ask or imagine (Ephesians 3:20).

Science tells us it takes *at least* 21 days to create a new habit. So, we purposely created this devotional and prayer journal to include both 21 days of devotions and 21 stories shared by others of their own unique faith hunts.

It's my prayer that these next 21 days do help initiate a new habit for you—the habit of being actively on the hunt for the Kingdom of God—of searching determined-

ly for more of Him, pursuing all He has planned for your life, and capturing all He has already promised you, and inspire you to have your very own Faith Hunt stories.

As you will see, the Kingdom not only works for hunting but also in every area of life! May this devotional and prayer journal be a tool to help you on your own life-changing journey.

Happy hunting!

—Gary Keesee

DAY 1
UNDERSTAND THE KINGDOM

But seek first the kingdom of God and His righteousness, and all these things will be given to you.

—Matthew 6:33

Are you actively hunting for the Kingdom of God?

The first step you should take, not just on your faith hunt but to see any real change in your life, is to learn more about the Kingdom of God. We have to change our mindsets when it comes to seeing supernatural results in our lives.

The supernatural is *natural* in the Kingdom, and it's all tied to God's Kingdom law. That's why we have to be spiritual scientists! We have to start asking questions like *"How did that buck show up?"* and *"How did that person receive healing?"*

We know God can't lie (Numbers 23:19), so one of the greatest questions we can ask is, "Why didn't I see what I was believing for in this area?" Some of the greatest lessons I've learned about the Kingdom of God have come from times when I sowed my seed for a deer and messed it up on my end.

Make sure you're taking time to study, write down, dissect, and understand the laws that govern the Kingdom of God.

You can do this by reading the Word, praying, and asking God for wisdom.

It's critical that you understand that God's Kingdom is established and upheld through justice, the administration of His law. Too many Christians are pleading with God for things He's already given them. Friend, the ball is in your court!

Second Corinthians 1:20 clearly says that every promise is "Yes" and "Amen." ALL of the promises of God are for you. It has already been decided; they are legally yours.

Once you learn what God says is legally yours as a citizen of His Kingdom, you need to learn how to lay claim to what is yours and release it in the earth realm.

If you know the law of God's Kingdom (His will), and you know that you have access to justice—the process of enforcement that guarantees you what the law says—then you can be confident and not afraid.

If you don't understand spiritual laws, you won't have the ability to enjoy their benefit or to duplicate them when you need them in your life or on your own faith hunt.

Seek all the knowledge you can regarding His Kingdom and how it operates, so you can access it and walk in it.

Today, _____(date), I commit to being intentional about seeking the Kingdom of God first. I will make time to prioritize prayer, read and study His Word, and listen to teachings. I will keep God and His Word at the forefront of my thoughts. I will ask Him to reveal to me how His Kingdom operates, my rights as a citizen, and how I can legally claim what is already legally mine!

Three promises from the Word of God that I am legally claiming are already mine as a citizen of the Kingdom of God are:

1. _____

_____

_____

2. _____

_____

_____

3. _____

_____

_____

"God's Word was written to instruct us, reveal Him and His ways to us, and to let us know the benefits of the covenant we have with Him. We need to believe His Word and release our faith in it in order to receive the benefits written there."

—Gary Keesee

My husband and I both had bear tags for the 2019 hunting season. I had limited time to go out and hunt, so I asked the Lord very specifically, saying, "I would like a medium-sized black bear who comes out, turns broadside, and moves slowly enough for me to get a good shot. I would also like it tonight when we go out hunting," and released my faith.

My husband picked me up after work, and we went out to our favorite "bear alley" to see what we could find. We normally stick to one main stretch of bush but decided to venture further out this time.

Around 8:30 p.m., a medium-sized black bear sauntered out about 100 yards in front of us. I knew without a doubt that this was my bear, and I was able to get a good shot.

The bear went down a steep incline, but stopped on a bench right before rolling down a cliff. Thankfully! We had a time dressing the bear out and backpacking it out of the steep area it was in while dodging the spines of the devil's club and rotten logs, but we made it just before dark. I was a very happy hunter! (And the bear bratwurst is superb!)

Many blessings to you all! I was looking for an opportunity to share how the Lord has used these Kingdom principles in our lives and to say "Thank You!" I love how He works!

—Grace G.

YOUR FAITH HUNT

Today's date: _____ Time: _____

Today, I prayed the prayer of faith for:

_____

_____

_____

_____

_____

_____

_____

_____

Date of answered prayer: _____

My Faith Hunt story:

_____

_____

_____

_____

_____

_____

_____

_____

_____

DAY 2
ARE YOU FULLY PERSUADED?

Against all hope, Abraham in hope believed and so became the father of many nations, just as it had been said to him, "So shall your offspring be." Without weakening in his faith, he faced the fact that his body was as good as dead—since he was about a hundred years old—and that Sarah's womb was also dead. Yet he did not waver through unbelief regarding the promise of God, but was strengthened in his faith and gave glory to God, being fully persuaded that God had power to do what he had promised.

—Romans 4:18-21

No matter where we are as believers, or what we've experienced with God, we can all use this refresher.

See, many Christians have had spiritual things happen in their lives, but they don't know how to duplicate them. They throw the word "faith" around fairly loosely, but they don't have a clear picture of what faith really is. They don't understand the laws of the Kingdom; they've just experienced them accidentally.

Romans 10:10 tells us that there are two things that must take place before heaven's authority and power can be released here in the earth realm.

1. You must be *fully persuaded* and be in agreement in your heart with what heaven says. This is faith.

When you're fully persuaded of what God says, anything contrary bounces off of you. If you're fully persuaded, when you close your eyes, you can see it.

2. You need to understand that being in faith by itself will not release heaven here.

Think of it like a light switch. The power is on, but you still have to flip the switch to turn the light on. In the same way, when you believe in your heart what heaven says that makes the connection with heaven legal or justified—the power is on. But then you have to *release* that authority here. You have to flip the switch on.

You do this as you confess and act on the Kingdom's authority.

Understanding this law of the Kingdom is VITAL to you having the ability to receive what heaven has for you. You will receive everything you will ever receive from heaven the same way you were saved—*by believing what heaven says in your heart and then speaking or acting on what heaven says.*

The laws of the Kingdom work every time, for anyone who will take the time to learn them and apply them. Just like electricity works the same in the United States as it does in Africa.

When Drenda and I really got this—when we discovered the switch and how to turn it on—*everything changed.*

That's what I want for you.

Today, _____(date), I commit to keeping the Word in my heart so that my heart will come into agreement with what heaven says and faith will be produced. I want to be fully persuaded of what heaven says so that I am able to release the authority of heaven in the earth realm by speaking it!

I am building faith in order to be fully persuaded of what heaven says in this area of my life:

_____

_____

_____

_____

_____

_____

_____

_____

_____

"For faith to exist, you must be fully persuaded
that God is going to do what He said He would do.
You have to take the time to become convinced, to
be in agreement with heaven...
in your heart."

—Gary Keesee

It was summer of 2014 when I was in a safety meeting
as a mine foreman and got the phone call that no
parent wants to get—my son had passed away due to
the opioid epidemic.

In August of 2016, I lost my job in the mines and was
spending a lot of time in the woods trying to keep my
mind occupied. I came home one evening and told
my wife I was aggravated that I was seeing bucks but
nothing of any size. I had several nice bucks on the trail
cameras but wasn't seeing them while in the woods. (I
have harvested many bucks over the years. One even
scored 143, so now I only hunt for big bucks.)

My wife told me I needed to "plant a seed."

At that time, I wasn't in church and didn't come from

a church family. I have always believed in the Lord Jesus Christ, but I didn't understand what she was saying. She explained to me that I needed to write a check and in the memo to put "deer harvest" for the assignment on the seed, and then we prayed the prayer of agreement.

Several days later, I had been in my stand for several hours and hadn't seen anything. I wanted to get down, but something kept telling me to stay still. That's when I saw movement. It was a buck! He was freshening up scrapes as he came around the flat! This gave me time to get into position and get ready to shoot. The buck came closer, stopped to freshen up another scrape, and by this time it was closer and I could tell it was a nice deer. As it continued around the flat, the deer was about 25 yards below me in the stand. I made a grunt sound with my mouth, and the deer stopped broadside.

I prayed, took the shot, and got a good hit. It was an 8-point buck!

I went home and told my wife. I was so excited to share what the Lord had given me! That's when my wife told me about a book she had bought me—Faith Hunt.

That was the start of my spiritual journey, which led to my salvation, water baptism, and baptism in the Holy Spirit. Faith Hunt was an anointed book the Lord used to minister to me. I read it from cover to cover and began to operate in the law of seedtime and harvest. I thank the Lord for the way He used this book to teach me in terms that I could understand.

—Jeff T.

YOUR FAITH HUNT

Today's date: _____ Time: _____

Today, I prayed the prayer of faith for:

_____

_____

_____

_____

_____

_____

_____

Date of answered prayer: _____

My Faith Hunt story:

_____

_____

_____

_____

_____

_____

_____

_____

_____

DAY 3
DOCUMENT YOUR
POINT OF CONTACT

Therefore when you pray, believe that you have received, and it will be yours.

—Mark 11:24

Sometimes you have to remind yourself of where you've been in order to have the victory where you are now.

In Mark 8:14, the disciples had forgotten to bring bread. Then Jesus started talking about leaven, and they thought He was saying that because they had no bread. But look at what He said next. He said, "Don't you remember?" Then He went on to remind them of their victories. Apparently, their victory—the answer to their fear and the issue they were facing—was in their *remembering*.

That's why you'll find a section after each day in this devotional for you to list the date and time and what you prayed for in faith. It's where you'll record your prayers and seeds sown—*your points of contact*—the defining moments when you released your faith.

Because nothing helps you defend your stand of faith as much as knowing exactly *when* you received by faith.

Oh, and you'll have to defend your stand of faith. Because you have an enemy, and he has a legal right to test you. He doesn't know your heart, and he wants to make sure that you don't get into agreement with heaven, because He knows that the only way that heaven can invade earth is if someone on earth comes into agreement.

So, when the enemy tries to say you haven't received yet, you can point to the exact day and time when God answered. Any time fear or doubt try to rise up, reflect back on the moment you prayed and released your faith and seed, encourage yourself in the Word, claim the promise of the Word, and stand strong!

The woman with the issue of blood defined her point of contact when she said, "If I can just touch the hem of His garment, I will be healed." When she touched Jesus, she drew on the anointing, her faith completed the circuit that allowed the power of God to flow to her, and she was healed.

There is also a section for you to record your *answered* prayers, so you can remember your victories and analyze the results that came from those victories. As you do, each of your personal "Faith Hunt" stories will become blocks in your foundation.

You'll find that there's nothing more encouraging to your faith and your family's faith than to write down a list of prayer requests, pray in faith over them, and watch God check them off the list as you're diligently seeking Him daily.

"Nothing helps us defend our stand of faith as much as knowing *when* we've received. When I pray the prayer of faith, I always note the time and day and then write it down."

—Gary Keesee

The Lord made it clear that He wanted us to move from Alberta to British Columbia in 2017. We were both surprised and unprepared financially for a move. This coincided with the Lord bringing Gary and his teaching into our lives.

We began to practice the principle of "sowing." I got Faith Hunt for my husband since he is an avid and successful hunter. We decided to sow for an elk. We ran into a problem, however. Because of our moving preparations in 2017, my husband had very little time to go hunting. He only went out a few times, and it was the only year since I have known him that he didn't get ANY animals (deer, elk, moose, or bear).

It appeared that no elk would be forthcoming. But then, one of my husband's hunting buddies came by our house and dropped off an elk because he didn't have time to process it before he went on vacation.

The elk showing up in such an unusual way emboldened me to sow for what I really wanted—a mortgage free house in BC. The Lord gave me the amount to sow and directed me where to sow it, then surprised me by instructing me to add "paid off car" along with "mortgage free house." So I did.

We had to go ahead with the mortgage and list our house in Alberta to meet our moving schedule. We had an older home, and although we kept it in good repair, there weren't many bites from interested buyers. I kept saying, "We only need one!" And that is what we got.

Only one couple looked at the house and bought it one month after it was listed. We had our mortgage in place for less than two months before we were able to pay it off and had enough left over from the sale of our Alberta home for a much needed and paid for new car.

—Grace G.

YOUR FAITH HUNT

Today's date: _____ Time: _____

Today, I prayed the prayer of faith for:

_____

_____

_____

_____

_____

_____

_____

_____

Date of answered prayer: _____

My Faith Hunt story:

_____

_____

_____

_____

_____

_____

_____

_____

_____

DAY 4
THE POWER OF
AGREEMENT

Again, truly I tell you that if two of you on earth agree about anything they ask for, it will be done for them by my Father in heaven. For where two or three gather in my name, there am I with them.

—Matthew 18:19-20

God created marriage and family; He has a divine purpose for both. He didn't just want you to have a few people to share household chores with or to go get ice cream with.

The Bible says to "be fruitful, fill the earth and subdue it." To subdue means to conquer and to bring under subjection. God's desire was that His administration and righteousness fill the earth.

God designed marriage and family so that the knowledge of His Kingdom would be passed on to future generations.

God wants each and every generation to know Him and serve Him more than the last. Serving the Lord is a very serious issue to our Father. In 1 Timothy 3, Paul tells Timothy that knowing how to lead and train our children is a prerequisite for promotion in God's Kingdom.

All prosperity starts at home—first with your marriage and then with your family.

But the devil has figured this out. He's caught on to what God wants to do with marriages and families, and he does everything he can to prevent that. He tries to bring pain, sorrow, and confusion into our marriages and families. He does whatever he has to do to erode righteousness and agreement and bring rebellion, because he knows, as God does, that there is nothing more powerful than a family that is aligned together with God's vision.

Agreement is incredibly powerful in the Kingdom of God. That's why Satan hates it. That's why he works so hard to cause division in marriages and families, and why you need to protect and fight for yours.

"If you're married, get into agreement with your spouse concerning a clearly defined picture, then release it into your life with your words."

—Gary Keesee

It was the 2017 season, and after a few seasons of successful faith hunts, I decided I wanted to take my faith to the next level as it pertains to deer hunting. I read Gary's book Faith Hunt several years prior and applied all the principles he encouraged us with and saw God's Kingdom work in some pretty amazing ways. I was excited for the next faith challenge, to say the least!

This season was going to be unique, because all of the private land I had previously had access to was now gone, so I was starting from ground zero.

While praying about the season, I felt I should trust God for a nice buck on the public game lands close to my house. I had never hunted or scouted the area I was planning to go to; I was just completely trusting the Lord.

On October 29, 2017, before I went out to hunt for the first time, I wrote out my declaration of faith: "Lord I come into agreement today, and I believe to receive a big 8-pointer on the game lands. Thank you for a clean harvest, in Jesus's name. Amen!"

After that, I sowed a seed to my local church and was ready to go. The piece of game land I was hunting was split up between two counties. Each county has their own set of rules you must follow. I was unaware of some of these rules and never checked before hunting because I was too excited to get out.

I decided to go without a stand and hunt with my rifle on the ground in one of the counties. After three hunts, I hadn't seen one deer. I didn't even see a rabbit! "Lord," I prayed, "I know your Kingdom works every time, so what am I doing wrong?"

As I prayed, the Lord brought to my mind the rules per county, so I decided to look them up. Come to find out, it's illegal to hunt from the ground in the county I was in. You must be at least eight feet off the ground to harvest a deer.

I remembered Gary saying that hunting illegally will stop the Kingdom. Aha! I knew what was wrong!

So on my fourth time out, I took my stand and climbed a tree. Still nothing! My faith was really being tested. I went back to the rule book, and after scanning all the rules, I prayed again and asked God to show me.

Instantly, the answer popped up: "Hunters must be 200 yards away from a dwelling to shoot a firearm on game lands." There it was. The fourth time I set up on the residential side of the game lands and was 100 yards from a home. No wonder I didn't see anything, I was hunting illegally again! From reading the rules, I found that I could hunt from the ground in the other county, so I decided that's what I would do.

Early in the morning on November 18, I sat under a random tree on the other county's side of the game lands. After sitting for about 10 minutes, and with the first rays of dawn peeking through, I heard a slight rustling to my right. I slowly turned my head to look, and about 30 yards away was a buck eating acorns. As I lifted my scope to take a closer look, I thought to myself, That's MY deer; that's the 8-pointer!!

Sure enough, when I scoped him, he was an 8-pointer! I worked to situate myself to get a clean shot. As I was doing that, the wind instantly changed and blew my scent right at him, and he took off. I tried to follow where he went but lost him as he went over the ravine. Not wanting to jump him too much, I decided to wait a few minutes before stalking him. Walking in the direction I saw him go, I kept my rifle up and stopped every few steps to scan the horizon of the woods in front of me. There were multiple trails he could have gone down, so I started praying, asking God to guide each step because I had no idea where he went.

As I went down one of the three trails, I continued my

strategy of stopping every few steps. It had now been well over an hour and a half since he took off, and I had walked well over 400 yards without any sign of the buck. My excited nerves had now turned to frustration. I needed to take a break, so I sat on a tree stump to rethink the situation.

As I was sitting there, I heard leaves crunching in front of me around 100 yards away. The sound was coming from behind a stack of dead trees, so I situated myself to peek around the pile.

When I put my scope up to look down the hill behind the pile, there he was 100 yards away eating acorns again! This was it! I had the perfect shot lined up. The safety was off, I calmed my nerves to steady the shot, and, boom, I took the first shot.

To my surprise, he was still standing there! I thought, Well, in 15 years of hunting, I've never shot a deer and had it just stand there. I must have missed him.

Frantically, I reloaded another round, this time shaking even more. Boom! Round two. At that point, the buck had started running in my direction but didn't look wounded.

I knew my scope was on. I had just sighted it in a few

days prior. It must be me, I thought. So, as he was running toward me, I kept my scope on him to give it one more try. I only had one more bullet left, so it was now or never. It was clear he wasn't stopping anytime soon, so I made a noise at him to get him to stop, and it worked! He stopped 40 yards in front of me perfectly broadside. Boom! Off went the third shot, and he disappeared.

Oh man, did I get him? I wondered. After the smoke settled, I took a closer look. There he was right where he had stopped. I was ecstatic, to say the least. I started jumping around shouting, praising God, thanking Him for the harvest and for His Kingdom.

What makes it even better was that this 8-pointer was the ONLY deer I saw in 5 hunts. God never misses a detail, and His Kingdom works every time! I, too, have learned this through deer hunting, like Gary, and have story after story just like this one to show for it. Thank you, Gary, for teaching us the Gospel of the Kingdom!
—Andrew T.

YOUR FAITH HUNT

Today's date: _____ Time: _____

Today, I prayed the prayer of faith for:

_____

_____

_____

_____

_____

_____

_____

Date of answered prayer: _____

My Faith Hunt story:

_____

_____

_____

_____

_____

_____

_____

_____

DAY 5
FAITH WORKS
THROUGH PATIENCE

Consider it pure joy, my brothers and sisters, whenever you face trials of many kinds, because you know that the testing of your faith produces perseverance. Let perseverance finish its work so that you may be mature and complete, not lacking anything. If any of you lacks wisdom, you should ask God, who gives generously to all without finding fault, and it will be given to you.

—James 1:2-5

Inheriting the promises of God requires faith and patience. Faith doesn't get nervous but expectantly waits for the manifestation of its hope.

In my hunting experiences now, the deer usually shows up my first time out and within 40 minutes. But that wasn't always the case.

Remember, God cannot lie. If there is a problem receiving from God, we need to examine the short circuit in our faith. Allow God to teach you and show you how faith works. Allow Him to show you how the process operates.

In Genesis 15, we see the story of Abraham. Early in the chapter, we see he believed God, but believing wasn't all there was to the process.

Abraham received the promise, but he still had to *do*

something. He had to act on his faith. And he had to *raise* Isaac.

See, the promise is different than the *maturity* of the promise. Sometimes we're so busy looking for the end result that we miss the birth of the promise.

Imagine if Abraham was so busy looking for a full-grown son that he missed the birth of Isaac, or refused to ever acknowledge the existence of Isaac until he was grown. But that's what we do as Christians! We miss ideas because we're looking for results. We want instant fixes. We either look at that baby of an idea and think it's puny, or don't acknowledge it at all because we can't get our eyes off the results.

But just like someone had to raise Isaac, and someone had to change his diapers, there is a process to faith. Sometimes it's messy and smelly and requires a whole lot of patience.

Don't get discouraged. When it's taking longer than you wanted, or when your faith seems to have failed, don't throw away your confidence in the Word of God.

Believe that when you pray and believe, you receive. Because faith is believing that you already receive what you're in the faith hunt for BEFORE it actually shows up.

And know that with faith and patience, the fruit of your faith will show up.

> "When you receive by faith, you know that you have it, and you wait in peace until it shows up in the physical world."
>
> —Gary Keesee

The kids and I were learning that as we give to God, God always gives back. I had been reading Faith Hunt by Gary Keesee and teaching it to my kids every night.

My 11-year-old son decided to give some of his money in the Sunday School offering. He was giving to God, expecting God to help him kill a bear this season. As for the rest of the family, we "knew 100%" we would get a bear. Since we kill one every year when we hunt in North Carolina, we didn't put our faith to work.

When we went to North Carolina that season, my son got his God-given bear. As for the rest of the family, we didn't get to tag a bear at all.

God's Kingdom principles work as long as you apply them!

—Loretta L.

YOUR FAITH HUNT

Today's date: _____ Time: _____

Today, I prayed the prayer of faith for:

_____

_____

_____

_____

_____

_____

_____

_____

Date of answered prayer: _____

My Faith Hunt story:

_____

_____

_____

_____

_____

_____

_____

_____

DAY 6

LIVE IN FULL
CONFIDENCE

Now faith is confidence in what we hope for and as-surance about what we do not see.
—Hebrews 11:1

What would you do if there was a $100 check from me, written out to you, tucked in the pages of this book?

I don't mean one of those pre-printed, marketing-tactic checks. I mean a *real* check—from my own personal or business account—written specifically to you for $100.

I'm guessing you'd cash it as soon as possible, right?

I'm also guessing that you'd think, *I have $100*, and you'd start thinking of how you were going to spend it. Despite that $100 check not being actual cash in your hand, you'd still see it as the *promise* of the cash, knowing that as long as you have that check, you'd have access to $100.

That's exactly how you should see the promises of God.

The problem is, as human beings, we have a tendency to want to wait for the proverbial cash to show up. We think we need to wait for God to *do* something in our lives *before* we say it. We've been trained to think, *I need evidence. Prove it.* So we do things like *hope* that we'll be able to start our own business someday, or *hope* that we'll receive our healing, or *hope* that we'll have a successful hunt.

But the promises of God will NEVER show up that way. That's not how the Kingdom flows into the earth realm. But we need to look at the "checks" that GOD Himself has *already* signed for us—His *precious promises!*

Since we know His character as a good and loving God, we must consider His promises finished even though we don't yet see the result. Second Corinthians 1:20 says, "For no matter how many promises God has made, they are 'Yes' in Christ. And so through him the 'Amen' is spoken by us to the glory of God."

Believe God's promises and speak them over your life. Act like you already have the evidence because He *already* gave you the promises, and He has the power to carry them through to completion.

Make the decision that you're going to have everything the Bible says you can have, and start calling things that are not as though they are TODAY.

> "Faith is the possession of something you can't see yet, knowing full well that you have it."
> —Gary Keesee

Several years ago during hunting season, I was sitting in church service, and the Holy Spirit laid it on my heart to go hunting with my husband like he'd been wanting me to (it had been more than eight years since I went deer hunting) that evening and to sow for a nice buck. As a farmer's daughter and sibling to hunters, one of my dreams had always been to shoot a nice buck. The Holy Spirit gave me an amount I should sow for a buck and where.

When we left church, I told my husband I'd go hunting with him. We got home and kind of rushed out the door to get in the tree stand before 2:00 p.m. I bought a tag that day. Roy had bought my license earlier in the year for me. I'm not a big time hunter. I only shot target practice twice in the two years leading up to this faith hunt, so sitting in my deer stand, all the odds started coming to my mind, and I struggled a bit with doubt.

Then I remembered I forgot to actually write the seed check before hurrying out to the deer stand! But God spoke to me and said, "Don't put me in a box; have faith. Write the check when you get home and simply receive from me now."

I relaxed and believed. Less than five minutes later, Roy (who was in the tree stand beside me) says, "There are two bucks behind you. Get ready."

I aimed, and Roy grunted to stop the bigger buck of the two in the clearing, and I took a shot. It was a very good hit, and my 8-point buck dropped just a couple of feet away.

That was my first time doing a faith hunt and my first time shooting a muzzle-loader, and it was awesome!!

—Malena M.

YOUR FAITH HUNT

Today's date: _____ Time: _____

Today, I prayed the prayer of faith for:

_____

_____

_____

_____

_____

_____

_____

_____

Date of answered prayer: _____

My Faith Hunt story:

_____

_____

_____

_____

_____

_____

_____

_____

_____

DAY 7
YOU WERE CREATED
TO WIN

The Lord will send a blessing on your barns and on everything you put your hand to.

—Deuteronomy 28:8

Take a minute and think back to the dreams you had for your life and your future when you were a child.

Wherever you are right now in life, you need to take a few minutes to remember those dreams. Because as little kids, we all played at victory. We didn't play divorce court or bankruptcy court or dead-end jobs. We played the superhero, the president, or whoever we looked up to. *We played at winning.*

You know why? Because God not only made you for success, but also He *marked* you for it.

You were created to win.

But sometimes we step out into things, and then life gets tough, and we think we've missed God. We have this weird idea that if we have fear or we face any problems or difficulties, then whatever we had set out to do must not have been from God.

But that's a lie from the enemy to get you to lose your confidence so you quit, or settle, and forget that God already marked you for success.

That's why you're going to have to *know* what God has promised you. You're going to have to know that He is faithful, that He has a plan, and that He's never caught off guard or taken by surprise.

If you're going to do anything great in your life, there is going to be pressure. There are going to be things that happen that don't look possible. You will have to make tough decisions. You will have to pass some tests. You will have to learn how faithful God is. You will have to practice the art of remembering that He is faithful and that He has marked you for success.

"Stay in faith (agreement) with what heaven says about you, about your situation, and about the Kingdom of God. Cast those thoughts that don't line up with what God says down like water off a duck's back."

—Gary Keesee

My mom and dad had me listen to the story about how your daughter believed for a Pomeranian puppy. I had been wanting a black and white female Shihtzu puppy. My mom said that she wanted a puppy that was at least seven months old that we did not have to potty train.

My parents prayed with me, and I sowed my own seed for my new puppy. I found a picture of what my new puppy would look like and put it as my screen saver. This way, I saw it multiple times every day. I would look online for my puppy, and my dad found several dogs that he thought I would like, but I knew exactly what I asked God for, and I did not want anything else.

One evening I found a lady selling a female Shihtzu online. The Shihtzu was in Tulsa, so I convinced my mom to hop in the car and drive the two and a half hours because I knew it was my dog. We met the owner, and as soon as I saw the puppy, I was in love! She was identical to the picture that I had on my screen saver!! And she was seven months old and was potty trained! God gave me the exact details that I had asked for! She cost only a fraction of the price of any other Shihtzu puppy I had seen! Baby Cakes is now a part of our family, and I will never forget what God did for me!!

I also believed the Lord for my first deer last year. I ended up shooting a small buck at the beginning of deer season with my Ravin Crossbow! My little brother turned six in November and did the same thing! He also killed a turkey this spring! God is awesome!!

—Sophi H.

YOUR FAITH HUNT

Today's date: _____ Time: _____

Today, I prayed the prayer of faith for:

_____

_____

_____

_____

_____

_____

_____

_____

Date of answered prayer: _____

My Faith Hunt story:

_____

_____

_____

_____

_____

_____

_____

_____

_____

DAY 8
THE POWER OF
A SEED

Give, and it will be given to you. A good measure, pressed down, shaken together and running over, will be poured into your lap. For with the measure you use, it will be measured to you.

—Luke 6:38

One of my favorite stories in the Bible is in Mark 6 where Jesus taught us how to release the Kingdom into our lives. There we read the story of Jesus feeding 5,000 men with just five loaves of bread and two fish. Maybe you know it, but basically, a large crowd was following Jesus, listening to Him teach, and watching Him perform miracles.

> *By this time it was late in the day, so his disciples came to him. "This is a remote place," they said, "and it's already very late. Send the people away so that they can go to the surrounding countryside and villages and buy themselves something to eat."*
>
> *But he answered, "You give them something to eat."*

Of course, Jesus knew the disciples would freak out. They couldn't feed 5,000 people. In fact, they started talking about how it would take more than half a year's wages to buy just a bite for that many people.

> *They said to him, "That would take more than half a year's wages! Are we to go and spend that much on bread and give it to them to eat?"*

Jesus was teaching the disciples how to release the Kingdom into the earth realm, and it started with Him asking them what they already had in their possession.

> *"How many loaves do you have?" he asked. "Go and see."*
>
> *When they found out, they said, "Five—and two fish."*

What do YOU have in your life that you can give God to work with?

Figure it out, and sow it. Sow into the Kingdom of God a portion of whatever it is you need. That's what the boy did with the bread and fish, and Jesus multiplied them.

Notice though that *bread multiplied to bread* and *fish multiplied to fish*.

That's how it works.

When something is given to the Kingdom, it is reproduced. The difference with money is that it's a bartering system, and money can be named. You and I "name" money every day. We name it "milk," "house payment," "gas," "bread," and anything else we need each day.

Money becomes whatever we need. Any money you give above your tithe can be named to be the thing you need multiplied.

Keep in mind that you can sow based on reason or based

on revelation. It takes little faith to sow by reason. Reason simply asks, "What can I afford?" Giving based on revelation means you determine your seed by praying, "Lord, what do you want me to sow?" This requires faith.

When you make your seed for your faith hunt a matter of prayer, your decision becomes an act of worship. Sowing by revelation is asking, "How much am I willing to trust God?"

> "I sow a seed, and then I am expectant, not because of my ability, but because I know that the law is operating for me. I can now receive whatever I have need of based on God's ability to work on my behalf."
>
> —Gary Keesee

In 2015, on the opening day of the firearms season in Indiana, as our group prepared to leave the vehicles for our stands, one of the hunters asked which deer I would be hunting for that day. We had a huge buck that we had named "Dualbeam" in the area of our hunting parcel, and we had him on trail cameras all year.

I answered "I am not coming out of the woods until I harvest Dualbeam!"

As I normally do in the wee hours before sunrise, I thanked God for giving me another morning and asked him to bless my family, friends, and the morning hunt! I also asked Him to give me a shot at Dualbeam!

The hunt started off well with many smaller bucks and does all around me that morning. Things slowed in the afternoon, and I even got out of the stand and took a small nap under the tree I was in.

At about 2:00 p.m., I climbed back into the stand and immediately had a nice 8-point come close to me. But I was waiting on Dualbeam. A long day in the stand started to look bleak for a harvest. With daylight wavering, I heard steps over my right shoulder.

A huge buck was freshening a scrape. He finally got within 60 yards of my stand, but with the low light conditions, I couldn't identify him. I finally decided I would shoot this buck.

With just three minutes of legal shooting light left, I pulled the trigger. I knew I hit the buck, and he ran in a circle and headed back out to an open field. After some time and getting my hunting companions together, we located the buck.

It was Dualbeam! God had delivered him to me at the last possible moment! This buck had a huge rack and scored 181-7/8 as a non-typical. The Lord absolutely delivered this buck to me! If you ask, you shall receive!!

—Phillip M.

YOUR FAITH HUNT

Today's date: _____ Time: _____

Today, I prayed the prayer of faith for:

_____

_____

_____

_____

_____

_____

_____

_____

Date of answered prayer: _____

My Faith Hunt story:

_____

_____

_____

_____

_____

_____

_____

_____

_____

DAY 9
DO YOUR PART

The Lord will send a blessing on your barns and on everything you put your hand to.

—Deuteronomy 28:8

Most of us have been taught that you sow and, with a wave of "God's magic wand," it's all done. But we have to know our part. We have to walk it out.

In Matthew 17, Peter went to Jesus and told Him he needed to pay their taxes. Jesus didn't tell Peter to "just have faith" to pay their taxes. No, Jesus gave Peter very specific instructions on how to get the money to pay their taxes. He had to go catch a fish and look in its mouth for the coin.

Getting the money to pay their taxes required more than faith. Peter had to *do* something. He had to act and act quickly.

God will present you with opportunities. That's what He does. It's your responsibility to have faith for those opportunities and to take advantage of them quickly when they come.

If you're going to run your race with Him, you're going to have to have faith, but you're also going to have to be proactive, prepared, and ready to do something.

Say I own a piece of land that has great potential to produce crops, but it's covered in weeds.

The potential is there, and I may feel called to farming, and I may have faith that the land will produce a huge harvest, but none of that matters if I don't take any action to get rid of the weeds.

So let's say that I declare war on the "kingdom of the weeds," and I take action and mow them down. Then, I have a beautifully cleared piece of land. Great, right?

Well, then I still have a part to play. I have to actually plant something good there or things still won't change on that land. Even though I have faith for the crops, I have to take the natural steps to plant the seed.

That's where so many Christians miss it. Unbelievers seem to know that getting a job done will require research and some work. But a lot of Christians think they get to skip the practical steps that are necessary on the natural side. They think they have a pass to jump ahead in the process—in *life*—simply because they feel called by God to something and have the faith for it.

But enjoying the promises of God takes more than faith. Prospering in the Kingdom takes both spiritual actions *and* natural actions. Having your own faith hunt story will REQUIRE that you get your hands dirty—that you *take action.*

By faith, we *see* what God has already given us, but we have to ACT on that revelation for it to have any impact here in the earth realm.

To see change in your life, to see answered prayers, to have your own faith hunt story, you have to have faith AND *do* something.

> "God can only bless the work of your hands. Your hands have to be doing something."
>
> —Gary Keesee

Hunting has been a passion of mine for more than 30 years. I've been a very successful hunter and haven't had to buy beef since 1997.

A friend lent me Faith Hunt in 2012, and I followed the principles of sowing a seed, being in agreement, and expecting my harvest. My friend told me to be very specific when praying, stating that God is a specific God. I prayed for a big buck, a wall hanger, that year and was blessed with the biggest buck of my life. I gra-

ciously thanked God, but a bit of me was wondering if it could've been a coincidence.

Well, in 2013 I again followed the principles in Faith Hunt but prayed for a bigger deer than the one I shot in 2012. Well, God came through and did, in fact, bless me with a bigger deer. In fact, it was and IS the biggest buck I've taken to date. It was a 200-lb., 10-pt. beautiful buck.

In 2014, realizing that money was tight and that I really couldn't afford to have another monster buck mounted, I planted seeds for two meat deer and a bear. (Keep in mind that in my 31 years of hunting, I've seen only a handful of bears and had never shot one.)

Well, God showed me that He is true to His word. Not only did I fill my tags for the deer I prayed for, but I also harvested my first bear, and it wasn't over bait. I was deer hunting with my bow when the bear came in and gave me a 12-yard shot!

God knows of my passion for hunting, and I believe He has used Faith Hunt to show me how faithful He is. He used my passion to catch my attention. I am blessed to have these testimonies that I share with people whenever I can.

I also realize that the principles in Faith Hunt can be used in all areas of our lives and that God will reach out to us in very personal ways to show us His presence. I've been wanting to share these testimonies with you, as well as to thank you for writing this book and making the principles so easy to understand.

—Raymond E.

YOUR FAITH HUNT

Today's date: _____ Time: _____

Today, I prayed the prayer of faith for:

_____

_____

_____

_____

_____

_____

_____

_____

Date of answered prayer: _____

My Faith Hunt story:

_____

_____

_____

_____

_____

_____

_____

_____

_____

DAY 10

ACCESS YOUR HELP

However, as it is written: "What no eye has seen, what no ear has heard, and what no human mind has conceived"—the things God has prepared for those who love him—these are the things God has revealed to us by his Spirit. The Spirit searches all things, even the deep things of God.

—1 Corinthians 2:9-10

Years ago, I was facing some obstacles. I had a dream one night that I was standing in the desert and in front of me was a straight road surrounded by flat sand. God said, *Walk down the road.* So I began walking.

Suddenly, huge cement barriers began to pop up here and there and completely block one side of the road or the other so that I had to dodge them as I walked. Then, someone came up behind me and put a blindfold on me. I questioned, "How am I going to walk down the road? I can't see where I'm going!"

God answered, *By My Spirit.*

That's how your life is supposed to be lived as a believer, friend—*by His Spirit.*

What does that really mean? *It means God wants to help you.*

It means He wants you to trust Him with your problems, with your questions, and with your needs. It means He wants you to walk in His power.

You have the right to be led in life by the Spirit of God. That's a whole lot better than you trying to figure it out on your own.

See, the Bible doesn't tell you who to marry, what degree to get, what occupation you should have, or exactly where you need to go to have your own faith hunt story. The Bible doesn't tell you whether or not you should buy or sell a house or buy or sell your stocks, or details like that.

But to be successful in life, you have to know those things.

And God *wants* you to know those things. He really does.

That's why He's given you access to some amazing help. The Bible tells us that the Holy Spirit is our Counselor. He's there to help you in life, in business, in your relationships, and with your faith hunt.

He's there to give you new ideas and plans that will take you to incredible places you've never been before, places that aren't familiar and may seem downright ridiculous to you, but not to Him.

You have access to things you don't know, things you've

never heard of, and things you've never thought of. You have an ability past yourself to succeed in every area of life—*through the Holy Spirit.*

"The Bible tells us that the promise comes by faith and it's guaranteed by grace. It's God's grace that does the work. It's not about you—it's about *you and God.*"

—Gary Keesee

Gary, I just wanted to relay my recent Faith Fishing Trip. I sowed a seed for a harvest of the limit of pink salmon on a local river here in Washington state. I've fished this river before and have only been able to catch one salmon even though I spent several hours on the river. (The legal limit is four.)

However, when I sowed a seed recently for a harvest of the legal limit of salmon, I went out "expecting" to catch my limit that day with God's blessing.

Within TWO hours, I had my FOUR salmon!

I was SO excited. Now, I'm about to go on a deer hunt-

ing trip, and of course, I sowed my seed for my deer. I have HIGH EXPECTATIONS that I will harvest my faith deer. I'll send you results when my hunt is over!

—Mike D.

YOUR FAITH HUNT

Today's date: _____ Time: _____

Today, I prayed the prayer of faith for:

_____

_____

_____

_____

_____

_____

_____

Date of answered prayer: _____

My Faith Hunt story:

_____

_____

_____

_____

_____

_____

_____

_____

DAY 11
HOW TO PRAY

Do not be anxious about anything, but in every situation, by prayer and petition, with thanksgiving, present your requests to God. And the peace of God, which transcends all understanding, will guard your hearts and your minds in Christ Jesus.

—Philippians 4:6-7

This is one of my favorite Scriptures on how we are to pray.

Notice that we are to ask *with thanksgiving*.

You can't be thankful about something you haven't received yet, right? You wouldn't send a thank you note in advance of someone giving you a gift or doing something for you, would you?

That's the lesson in this Scripture. We receive what we're asking God for by faith, so we're to be thankful because we KNOW that we've *already* received.

That means you should be thanking Him for all He's *already* done and for what He's *about* to do in your situation and in your life. You should be thanking Him *before* your answer shows up, because He's faithful and good.

In Judges 20:19, we read about the nation of Israel suffering great loss after a huge battle; they had lost 22,000 men. Can you even imagine? I'm sure you'll agree that that was a really bad day.

Then, on the second day of battle, they lost 18,000 more men. The Bible tells us they took a day off at that point. They needed to regroup. Then, in verse 26, we see that the entire army presented offerings of thanksgiving to God.

Why would they present offerings of thanksgiving in the midst of such terrible defeat?

Because they needed to remind themselves that God was FOR them, that He was with them.

What about you?

When was the last time you reminded yourself that God is *for* you, and *with* you; that His grace is sufficient; that He is your help; and that He is faithful and good?

> "If you know what God has already given you, you don't need to 'ask' in the sense of wondering if you're going to get a positive answer. Instead, you can 'ask' like a person turning in a requisition, placing a draw on something that has already been given."
>
> —Gary Keesee

I read your Faith Hunt book last summer. My wife and I sowed seed for a deer, specifically a "good tasting" deer. I love venison, but my wife wasn't sure, so I wanted a good tasting one so she wouldn't be turned away from it.

I attempted to go hunting during gun season but didn't have time. My friends all talked to me and recommended bow hunting. I've never hunted with a bow in my life. I did a little research and bought two Barnett Jackal crossbows.

Still kind of unsure about it, I sighted in the bow at an archery range. My wife and I were in agreement, and we continued to proclaim that we would receive the deer.

Early in November, I asked an acquaintance if I could hunt on his farm. He said yes and recommended a spot. On November 20, I went out to bow hunt on my own for the first time. I sat in a blind that he said I could use for awhile.

An hour and a half passed, and it was getting dark. I was running out of time. I kept praying and saying "I know my deer is out here." But I didn't see or hear any deer.

I remembered a story from your book where you said you got a deer on the way back to your vehicle. I said to myself, My deer is here, and I'm not leaving without it. Then I began to walk slowly and cautiously back to my vehicle.

After walking about 100 feet, I looked across an open cornfield and spotted my deer. Unfortunately, the deer was over 200 yards away. I said, "That was my deer," very quietly and began to walk toward the deer.

Of course, the deer was slowly walking away from me, nibbling at the ground as it went. I spoke to that deer and said "In the name of Jesus, deer, you will turn around and head back my direction!"

To my joy, the deer did exactly that. I continued to stalk this deer across an open field, walking toward it only when its head was down. I covered about 150 yards, until I was about 50 yards from the deer. I knew that I had sighted in the bow at 20 yards and that my lowest pin would be about 45 yards. I told the deer to stop and it did, giving me two perfect broadside shots. I got a few steps closer, aimed in, added a little Kentucky windage and said "Lord, I need your help with this shot." I aimed in, exhaled, and pulled the trigger. I heard a whack and looked over to see that I had hit the deer. It only ran about 30 feet before collapsing.

> *I went up to the deer and discovered that not only did I hit the deer in a good spot, but also it was the best possible shot—through the shoulder, heart, and lungs. I was jumping for joy and thanking God for this wonderful deer: a good-for-eating button buck!*
> —Nathan R.

YOUR FAITH HUNT

Today's date: _____ Time: _____

Today, I prayed the prayer of faith for:

_____

_____

_____

_____

_____

Date of answered prayer: _____

My Faith Hunt story:

_____

_____

_____

_____

_____

DAY 12

KEEP RENEWING
YOUR MIND

Do not conform any longer to the pattern of this world, but be transformed by the renewing of your mind. Then you will be able to test and approve what God's will is—his good, pleasing and perfect will.

—Romans 12:2

You have an enemy, and you had better know his tactics.

But, most of the time, our problem isn't the enemy—it's our lack of understanding. We give too much credit to the enemy. If we really understood the truth and the authority we have, we'd know exactly how to fight back and take territory.

We can't really know the truth without really knowing the Word of God.

First John 5:14 says that the confidence we have in Him is that if we ask anything according to His will, He listens and hears us. But if you don't know the will of God, you can never be confident. And if you're not confident, you can never take territory.

You have to renew your mind to the Word of God. How? Read your Bible.

Test every thought you have against God's will for you. How do you know His will? *The Bible.* Measure everything against what God says. Umpire your thoughts. If they don't line up with what God says, get them out! Replace them with right thoughts.

You have to know how to build your house on the rock. You have to know the Word and stay in agreement with what God says. You have to cast aside thoughts that are coming at you that don't line up with the Word. You have to be courageous enough to wade into the face of circumstances—into the pressure—and declare the Word over situations.

Because there *will* be pressure.

Satan wants to tempt you to run back to where you think it's safe. He wants you to forget who you are and everything God has promised.

You're just going to have to be confident that you can take it because, many times, the victory is based on that—on whether or not you can hold on to it under pressure.

This is why I say that memory verses aren't just for kids; they're for everyone.

If you memorize Scriptures, you'll have them ready and waiting to replace negative thoughts.

When Drenda and I started changing our thoughts, she

put Scriptures and the promises of God *everywhere*.

She said, "I used to run into the bathroom when I felt depressed or when I was throwing myself a pity party. It was my only quiet place, so I put Scriptures there."

We both needed constant reminders that we wouldn't be in the wilderness forever. We were going through a hard time, but we were going *through*—we weren't staying there. We were headed somewhere else, somewhere better. We knew God had promises for our family. The Word of God was working in our hearts and minds. We were learning how to access the Kingdom inside of us by renewing our minds.

See, Satan fears the Word. He fears the living Word of God. He knows that if your spirit incubates the Word, there's no stopping it. It will produce *every time*. So the only thing he can do is bring pressure against you to make you give up—to make you let go of the Word; to make you think it can't be done; to make you think it's too hard, too scary, or too late.

You will face problems. You're not going to escape life without something negative happening. Life is full of things we don't see coming. But the Bible says when those days come, hold your ground.

It's what you do in those moments that will determine the outcome of your life.

"We must hear with our spirits (hearts) for faith to be present. Only the Word of God is able to affect the hearts of men. It requires a process of continual renewal."

—Gary Keesee

My wife and I agreed in prayer that I would get a deer and that my friend who needs deer meat would get two deer. We were specific in praying that we would get our deer in the morning on opening day. And we prayed for accurate shots.

We confessed that we had the deer exactly as we had prayed, and we released our faith. I was confident that we had received what we had prayed.

That morning, I went to my friend's woods after daybreak. I went out to a nice spot. As I looked to my rear at about two o'clock, there was a new tree stand with a hunter in it. He was on private land, and there was a fence between us. He was probably about 80 yards out. I decided to move out of his range.

Shortly after that, a deer came out of some brush

about 50 yards out. I had a shotgun with a rifled barrel and a Burris 50mm scope on it. I took the shot, and the deer ran off. Another deer appeared in the same area. I mounted my gun on a tree and fired. The deer dropped right on the spot. As I looked up on the hill, about 70 yards up the hill, the other deer had stopped and stood broadside.

I mounted my gun on the tree again and dropped that deer too.

When I approached the first deer I had shot, about 10 feet right behind her was another deer that my friend had been tracking. I gave my friend one of the deer, and we got exactly what we had prayed.

Two weeks later, after gun season ended, I prayed and agreed with my wife that I would shoot a deer in our backyard, as we lived in the country. But we rarely see deer, especially after gun season.

That Saturday, I got up and as I was eating breakfast, I looked out of our bay window and saw a buck standing broadside. I stood there in my p.j.s and bathrobe and looked at him since I really wasn't ready to deal with the deer. I had just woken up and wanted to relax and have breakfast. But then I thought, Well, I did pray, and this deer is just standing there. I debated it back and forth.

The deer was still standing there after several minutes, so I thought it must be a God thing for it to still be there. I decided to get my crossbow out of the garage. It is an Excalibur Recurve. It's not an easy job to cock it, but it outshoots most crossbows for power and distance.

As I went to pull the string back on the crossbow, I could not cock it. Finally, after three tries, I was successful. As I walked in front of the bay window on the way to the door, I could see that the deer was (amazingly) still there. By walking in front of the window, I could have also scared most deer away, but this deer just stood there.

I opened up the back patio door slowly and crept out to the edge of the doorway. I placed my crossbow up against the doorframe and scoped in on the deer at 50 yards. I pulled the trigger on the bow, the bolt released, and the limb on the bow glanced the side of the door, throwing my shot off. The deer grunted and then ran off.

I looked for the bolt and found it had plunged into the side of a tree. The broadhead was buried. The trajectory and flight of the arrow would have been a kill shot had not the crossbow limb glanced the side of the door.

Later, my nephew and I dug out the broadhead, and I shared with him the testimonies of how the Lord can provide.

—Dan A.

YOUR FAITH HUNT

Today's date: _____ Time: _____

Today, I prayed the prayer of faith for:

_____

_____

_____

_____

_____

Date of answered prayer: _____

My Faith Hunt story:

_____

_____

_____

_____

_____

DAY 13
WATCH YOUR
WORDS

The tongue can bring death or life; those who love to talk will reap the consequences.
—Proverbs 18:21 (NLT)

When you talk, you're releasing power into your situation—for good or for bad.

Now, that can work in your favor. But if you aren't using your words wisely, it can cause you a lot of trouble down the road.

When some people pray, their perspective is that it's like writing a letter of requests to Santa Claus. People don't realize that God already gave them the keys of the Kingdom, and they are *always* releasing the Kingdom through their *words.* Matthew 18:18 says, "Truly I tell you, whatever you bind on earth will be bound in heaven, and whatever you loose on earth will be loosed in heaven."

Wow! Did you get that? Whatever *you* bind on earth will be bound in heaven.

That means that you directly control the blessing in your life.

That gives a whole new revelation to the power of your words, right?

So if blessing is being short-circuited in your life, guess who is binding that blessing? And if unfortunate circumstances are overrunning your life, guess who is loosing permission for Satan to attack?

Yep. You.

Step back and think about what you're saying. Don't say, "Well, I've tried that 'faith stuff,' but it hasn't worked." Don't say you don't trust God or you're not seeing results. Make sure that you're not decreeing junk!

The law of releasing life or death in your life is in the power of your tongue, and it is operating all the time. Your words are a weapon. Are you using them against Satan, or against yourself and other people?

That's a sobering thought, but it's meant to be positive. Think of what you can decree! Don't fear that authority. Rejoice in it! Speak good things. Use your words wisely. Say "yes" and "amen" to every promise. Decree provision, healing, direction, wisdom, and health. Decree your faith hunt story!

"The Kingdom of God is released with a believing heart and a faith-speaking tongue."
—Gary Keesee

I was first introduced to your ministry through Fixing the Money Thing, where you had mentioned learning faith through deer hunting. Being a deer hunter myself, that caught my attention. Although I have been blessed through the years with many successful hunts, I had never given any serious thought to using faith for a deer. (Of course, I've had those moments of, "Oh, please, please, please..." but they don't work.) After hearing your hunting stories, here is what I did.

While hunting the late 2012 muzzle-loader season in Indiana, I saw a nice buck. Indiana has a one-buck rule and I had already harvested a buck, so this guy was off limits. I sowed a seed into your ministry saying, "I receive 'that' buck with my muzzle-loader, out of a certain ladder stand during the 2013 deer firearm season. Lord, protect and nurture 'that buck for me.'"

In firearm season 2013, I took my muzzle-loader, got in that stand, used a doe bleat call three times, and before I could put the call down, "that" buck came walking up the hill to me.

Later, as I was taking pictures of my harvest, I was assaulted with the thought of, Are you sure that is the same deer you saw last year? You know you didn't get that good of a look. This was true. I didn't get a good look and couldn't honestly say 100% that was him. The deer I had seen in 2012 had a unique left side antler, as did this deer I harvested. But I believed it was him because I had sowed for "that" buck. But to prove it really works, I figured I'd do it again!

Twenty-fourteen turkey season: My son and I have hunted together since he was old enough (he is now 36). We have been blessed with many deer and turkey harvests. I have hunted almost exclusively with a flintlock muzzle-loader for deer and turkey for several years. My son had never had the occasion to witness a flintlock turkey kill.

I sowed into your ministry for a long beard with my son as a witness. Our morning hunt was a bust. Later, after we had relocated and were discussing what to do next, a long bearded turkey came walking along the field edge into the woods straight to us.

Now, usually, we set up and call to the turkey. Not this time! I stood with my son standing behind my right shoulder, looking pretty much right down the gun barrel with me, and watching as I shot that bird. That had us both pretty excited. "Better than I could ask or think!" Praise the Lord; this is fun!

Twenty-fourteen deer archery season: For the past

several years, my son has had the opportunity to manage some acreage for hunting. He places game cameras on the property to see what kind of deer are using the property. He will give names to some of the bucks based on the configuration of their antlers.

In the 2014 season, he had a couple of nice 10-pointers, a really nice 12-pointer, and various 8-pointers. One particular 8-pointer had a rack of a fashion which earned him the name "Lobster."

As my wife and I prayed for me to receive a deer, she asked which one I was claiming. I said, "10-pt or better." She said, "That's not very specific."

"Okay," I said. "I receive Lobster. He's very unique. There's no mistaking him."

I went hunting that night with my crossbow. As I was watching five does right in front of my stand, Lobster walked out on top of the hill, too far away. He seemed content to stay where he was. As I "patiently" waited and reminded myself that I had already received this deer, a nice heavy-beamed 8-pointer came from behind me and stood 15 yards in front of me. That was more than Lobster could take. Down he came and ran junior off. But he was too fast for a shot.

He then began to chase the does. Up and down, back and forth, here and there, around and around. The 8-pointer came back and stood right in front of me. Lobster was back on top of the hill. Now, every memory I had of a big deer that I didn't get began to play in my mind.

As loud as I dared with an 8-point buck standing 15 yards in front of me, I said to the memories, "No!" and to Lobster, I said, "I sowed for you. Now get down here!"

As I spoke, a doe walked out in the clearing at about 20 yards. Lobster turned, came down the hill, ran off the 8-pointer again, and started toward the doe. I shot him at 20 yards. First-time crossbow kill! This is fun!!!!

Although these are just hunting stories to some, to me they are life lessons. Believe that you receive, and if it looks like it's not going to come to pass, then speak to it with a heart of faith, or as you teach, with agreement.

Isaiah tells us that God says that His Word will accomplish the purpose for which it was sent. As you teach, it would be perverse to say anything else. Thank you for your teaching!

I used the same, "I sowed for you, now get over here" on a turkey this past turkey season. I saw him at about 350 yards away with a hen. He seemed content to stay with her. After I spoke to him, she (the hen) ran him off. He crossed the distance to me. He had three beards. I had never harvested a multi-bearded turkey before. It's quite a trophy!

I've used these hunts to help show my family that faith in God really works. Prayer works, and we can receive an expected end. My son sent me pictures of some really nice bucks that are on his property this year. He said, "Get your checkbook ready!" He was referring to sowing for the deer I wanted.

—Keith T.

YOUR FAITH HUNT

Today's date: _____ Time: _____

Today, I prayed the prayer of faith for:

_____

_____

_____

_____

_____

_____

_____

_____

Date of answered prayer: _____

My Faith Hunt story:

_____

_____

_____

_____

_____

_____

_____

_____

DAY 14
DON'T WAVER

Truly I tell you, if anyone says to this mountain, "Go, throw yourself into the sea," and does not doubt in their heart but believes that what they say will happen, it will be done for them.

—Mark 11:23

One of the most important lessons God taught me concerning how faith works happened way back in 1993. I shared the story in *Faith Hunt*—about "The List" for tagging deer that were hit on the road, but it's critical that you understand the significance, so I'm touching on it again here.

I shared how I got on that list, thinking it would be a great way to get extra venison. And it was. Before deer season ever began that year, I had already butchered five deer.

Here's the thing though: because we were stocked up, I wasn't excited to go hunting. In fact, I went into the season without even praying or asking God for my deer. And I didn't sow any seed either.

Being on the list had affected my faith and divided my focus.

The list was a backup plan.

I knew in the back of my mind that if my faith in God didn't come through with a deer, I could always get one from the police department.

My faith was divided. I had two completely different visions of how to get my needs met. Without realizing it, I had believed in my own method (the roadkill list), and yet I *wanted* to trust God to bring my deer through hunting.

I was wavering in where I placed my trust, and I ended up receiving for two years from where I had the most confidence—the list. My faith had operated, but not how I had wanted it to.

The Bible says a man who is double-minded should expect to receive nothing from the Lord. But we can easily do this without even thinking. (Have you ever asked God to meet a need and believed you'd pay cash for it, but figured you'd just use a credit card if He didn't come through in time?)

Sarah and Abraham had a backup plan. Remember them? God promised He would give them a son. But things were taking a little too long. In Genesis 16, we see that Abraham and Sarah grew weary and began to doubt God would fulfill His promise. So, they took matters into their own hands. And Ishmael was conceived by Abraham and Sarah's servant, Hagar.

God still fulfilled His promise, but Abraham and Sarah had made life a lot harder on themselves by going with their Plan B instead of trusting God and His timing.

Faith doesn't need a safety net. If you have a backup plan, you're not walking in faith. And you'll always find that your alternative plan is really the one you're trusting.

As humans, we like to have everything in place so we feel secure. But God wants us to realize that there is no place more secure than resting in faith.

> "God does not change. Learn to trust Him to come through, and don't prepare backup plans for the 'what ifs.'"
>
> —Gary Keesee

I am a 14-year-old boy that has been intrigued by your book Faith Hunt. I live in Colorado and come from a long line of hunters. My family and I hunt deer, elk, and occasionally, antelope.

Last year, I shot a little 4-point deer, which made me positive for a deer this year. That was my second tag, and until my mom had me start reading your book, I had never thought about God helping me fill my tag.

I have been on plenty of hunts where we walked 11 miles a day and didn't see anything but a squirrel and some birds the whole time.

As I was reading your book, I felt a stirring and excitement to try what you were teaching on. So I sowed my seed for an 8-point buck, a clean shot, and that we wouldn't have to follow a blood trail or wonder if I hit a major organ. The rest of the week, I prayed and thanked God for my deer.

My tag started on October 28th and lasted for 10 days. My dad and I went hunting the first 6 days and saw 4 does and a buck on restricted property. The next morning, I was reading your book and it all of a sudden hit me—every time you sowed your seed, you agreed with your wife. I hadn't agreed with anyone for my deer, and that was why my seed wasn't producing fruit.

So I re-sowed and agreed with my family for my 8-point buck. We didn't hunt for the next 2 days. We went out expectant the next morning, and I harvested an 8-point white-tail mule/deer cross in just 15 minutes and at 150 yards. God answered my prayers for a clean shot, and he dropped where he was standing. God blessed me with what I asked of him.

But He didn't stop there! My dad was talking to one of his friends the next day about my deer and his odd characteristics. His friend has a buddy that's a white-tail mule/deer crossbreed expert that has studied them for awhile. Come to find out, my deer is a very rare crossbreed!

—Matthew G.

YOUR FAITH HUNT

Today's date: _____ Time: _____

Today, I prayed the prayer of faith for:

_____

_____

_____

_____

_____

_____

Date of answered prayer: _____

My Faith Hunt story:

_____

_____

_____

_____

_____

_____

DAY 15
LIVE THE PROMISES

Then Peter began to speak: "I now realize how true it is that God does not show favoritism."

—Acts 10:34

What does your life say to the people around you who don't know God?

If you didn't know Him and you saw someone who did know Him that lived a life like yours, would you *want* to know Him?

At a conference in Virginia Beach years ago, I met a young woman who had asked herself those very questions. She told me, "A year ago, I was thinking, 'I can't even tell people about God, because why would they want my God? Why would they want what I have?" Because, a year before, she was $45,000 in debt, had only a part-time job, both of her kids were sick and needed to go to the doctor, her husband was out of work, and they needed a place to live. Everything was coming to a screeching halt for her.

But when she saw me at that conference, she started shouting and jumping. She came up and gave me a hug and thanked me, and acted like she'd known me for a long time. She shared how she had heard our story and she had gotten some of our CDs. She listened to the CDs, began to apply the principles, and now she has an amazing story of how she paid all the debt off, and everything changed. They started a business. They paid for the business. They bought a house and paid for it.

Her whole life changed in 12 months. She was excited. And, she had brought a group of ladies with her to the conference, because they were seeing the results in her life and they wanted some for themselves.

It's our job to show people the true character of God, how His principles apply to everyone—how we can all live the promises of God.

Now, don't get me wrong. I understand that you might be facing some of the toughest situations of your life right now, but I'm here to tell you that the laws of the Kingdom work for ANYONE. They WILL work for YOU.

But you have some work to do. You have to change the way you think about your life. You have to change the way you think about the Word of God. You have to start engaging.

Write down the visions and dreams you have, not just for your faith hunt but for YOUR LIFE. Then, release your seed, water it with words of faith, and cause it to mature by keeping your eyes on the promise and staying in a place of believing God regardless of the storms you may see or the struggle you face today. Be encouraged! It may be plowing time now, but you will come to harvest day and it will be worth it!

Do as God said in Malachi, "Test me in this and see if I will not open the windows of heaven and pour out a blessing that there shall not be room enough to contain."

> "We are the ones who control the harvest in our lives. It's our faith in the laws of God that determine our ability to operate in the laws."
> —Gary Keesee

Our family was in Alaska on vacation. The fact that we were even there was a dream for me.

One day as we were driving around in the Kenai Peninsula, we noticed a huge fish hanging outside a charter boat on a rack. Most of the charter boats had just come in; and up and down the harbor, these same big fish were hanging. I had never seen a halibut before at the time, and I didn't know what they were, but they were huge. We were amazed as we passed charter after charter, all advertising a day's fishing for halibut.

Suddenly, Drenda turned to me and said, "I would like to catch a halibut, and I would like to catch one with that captain right there." She pointed to a sign advertising a halibut fishing charter that had the Christian symbol of the fish on the sign.

I was shocked! Drenda had never wanted to fish before. But she insisted, so we went into the office. Inside, we saw a sign that was talking about a Halibut Derby that was in progress, but soon would be coming to a close. The Halibut Derby is a contest among all the charter captains to see who can catch the biggest halibut. The winner would get their picture in the paper and a check.

Drenda and I talked about entering the Derby since we were going out anyway. It was only a few dollars to enter.

Drenda turned to me and said she decided that she was going to win the Derby so that that specific captain's business would get the recognition among all the charter captains because he was a Christian, and God would get the glory.

So when our turn came up to sign up at the desk, Drenda boldly declared that she was going to win the Halibut Derby so that God would get the glory and their business would be recognized because they were a Christian business. I'm sure the charter boat captain had heard that before, but I'm not sure he had heard anyone declare that they were going to win the derby for the glory of God.

He didn't say much.

We went out and began fishing, and we immediately started catching halibut. Every time she caught one, Drenda would ask the captain, who was also the owner, how big the halibut had to be to win the derby. He said the 40-pounder she caught wasn't big enough, so we threw it back. He said the 70-pounder she caught wasn't big enough.

The day continued toward evening, and it was now turning to dusk. My son Tom, daughter Polly, and I all had reached our two-halibut limit. Drenda had her 70-pounder, but none of the fish we had on board would win the derby.

Drenda still was confident she was going to catch "the big one." The captain told all of us to reel our poles in, as it was time to head to dock. Drenda ignored the order as the captain helped all of us put our poles up and stow the gear. She begged for just a few more minutes as she again declared that she WAS going to catch the derby-winning fish. The captain waited a few minutes, then finally said, "I'm sorry, but we really need to be going."

Just before he reached for her pole, it took a sudden downturn. The rod bent over, and the drag began to scream. The captain lifted the pole to get a feel for how big the fish was. He suspected it was a shark, and said he could tell by the way the fish pulled.

It was a big fish.

It took quite a while for Drenda to get that fish up. It took all her strength to reel that fish in. Finally, as the fish surfaced, everyone could see that it was actually a very big HALIBUT, one that was bigger than Drenda herself.

As the fish was pulled to the boat, the captain had a special prod that was designed for such big fish, so it wouldn't hurt any of the passengers or damage the boat. As he pushed the prod against the fish's head, the fish jerked, causing the charge to miss and the fish to dive back into the water.

All 300 feet of the line screamed off the reel. I didn't think the line or the hook were going to hold.

Drenda had to pull that bigfishupagain. Sinceshe had already wrestled the fish up once, she was struggling. I put my arms around her, putting my hand on the reel with hers, and we both slowly cranked it up to the surface again. This time the captain was able to get it in the boat, and we all marveled at its size.

That halibut weighed 123 pounds. It was longer than Drenda.

Drenda won the Halibut Derby.

Nothing is too small or unimportant to bring under the dominion of the Kingdom. The Kingdom of God should be impacting EVERY area of your life, but YOU are the one who has to release the provision that you need or want into your life. It won't just happen by itself.

YOUR FAITH HUNT

Today's date: _____ Time: _____

Today, I prayed the prayer of faith for:

_____

_____

_____

_____

_____

_____

_____

_____

Date of answered prayer: _____

My Faith Hunt story:

_____

_____

_____

_____

_____

_____

_____

_____

_____

DAY 16
MOVE FORWARD IN
THE FACE OF FEAR

Be strong and courageous. Do not be afraid or terrified because of them, for the Lord your God goes with you; he will never leave you nor forsake you. Then Moses summoned Joshua and said to him in the presence of all Israel, "Be strong and courageous, for you must go with this people into the land that the Lord swore to their ancestors to give them, and you must divide it among them as their inheritance. The Lord himself goes before you and will be with you; he will never leave you nor forsake you. Do not be afraid; do not be discouraged."

—Deuteronomy 31:6-8

If you know anything about my story, you know that years ago I had real issues with fear.

Growing up, I was painfully shy and insecure. I survived life by withdrawing. In fact, my plan was to just get done with high school and live in the woods, away from people.

I hadn't learned how to handle fear, so fear was handling me.

God had to fix me. He had a specific purpose for my life, and He wanted to help me get there. When I was 19 years old, God called me in a vision to preach—*to people*. So I *had* to change. After all, a preacher who is afraid of people would live a miserable, unproductive life. There was only one answer: I had to have courage. I had to move forward in the face of fear again and again and again. I had to keep moving forward to get where He wanted me to go.

Friend, YOU have to learn how to move forward in the face of fear.

You have to learn how to handle fear so fear doesn't handle you.

That's what Satan loves to set up—**F**alse **E**vidence **A**ppearing **R**eal—smoke screens and setups and shadows that all seem much bigger and scarier than they really are.

Why? Because he despises us, and he's not playing games. He wants to take us out. He wants to stop the Kingdom of God from manifesting, and he wants to hinder the plans of God for *your* life.

So he pushes your buttons. He knows what to say to make you afraid. After all, you've been trained by our culture to fear. Fear permeates our culture. Movies, television, news reports—they've all helped train us to fear or to react to circumstances in fear.

That's why 1 Peter 5:8 says, "Be self-controlled and alert.

Your enemy the devil prowls around like a roaring lion looking for someone to devour."

But you don't have to fear the enemy or evil, friend.

It doesn't matter how weak you feel or how afraid you are. God said He will NEVER leave you nor forsake you.

You can be courageous not because of who *you* are, but because God is with you.

Psalm 23:4 says, "Even though I walk through the darkest valley, I will fear no evil, for you are with me; your rod and your staff, they comfort me."

See that? *God is with you.*

So, as a believer, the real battle against fear occurs in your mind. That's the only way Satan can gain entrance. That's why you have to take your thoughts captive. You have to draw the line. You have to stand your ground.

You have to have courage.

That doesn't mean that you won't face fear. No, courage is actually defined as the mental or moral strength to venture, persevere, and withstand danger, fear, or difficulty.

Courage is moving forward in the face of fear.

God has called you to be strong and courageous, to confront the lies, the insecurities, the inferiorities, and the intimidation of the enemy. Don't believe **F**alse **E**vidence **A**ppearing **R**eal. God is with you.

> "You can be in faith or you can be in fear. Even when you think you're in faith, sometimes your mind will still yak at you in fear. Don't let it take root. Tell it to shut up. Cast those thoughts aside. Don't act on those fears or release fearful words."
> —Gary Keesee

We recently took a family vacation to Cocoa Beach/ Cape Canaveral, Florida. My husband wanted to go on a deep sea fishing boat and hopefully bring some fish home, back to Colorado. We had been planning the trip for a few months, so when he told me that he wanted to go fishing, I got excited and said, "Let's do it! And let's believe God for a great catch!"

I asked him what kind of fish were available in Florida where we were fishing. Of all the fish he rattled off to me, I chose to pray and believe for the giant red snapper.

The day came and we were waiting to get our instructions from the boat captain and crew. I had been confessing that I was going to catch a giant red snapper, so my excitement grew as the captain spoke. I was disappointed to hear the captain say that currently the only fish we wouldn't be able to keep were bass, flounder, and red snapper. Ugh, I thought; what else is there to believe for?

Well, I wasn't going to pass up this opportunity to work my faith. I said, "Lord, I have been believing for a giant red snapper, and so be it, I am going to catch one and still bring some kind of fish home!"

So while on the boat, I turned to my 8-year-old daughter and said, "Remember that you can pray and believe God that you'll catch a fish today. Do you believe?" She smiled and nodded her head in agreement. I said the same words of encouragement to my 21-year-old daughter. She flashed me a look of surprise but then agreed. I looked at my husband and said, "Let's believe for a big catch!"

A few hours went by and nothing hit on our lines that stayed. Then suddenly, my 8-year-old daughter's line got hit and she got so excited. She called out to her father to help her. A few minutes later, they pulled in an Atlantic shark! Wow, Rachel got the belief thing! So we commended her. What a trouper!

I remember beginning to think I might not get any-thing, but I stopped the thought and confessed that I already had my fish. I sat down and relaxed and heard God say, "If you just relax and let me bring the fish to you, you'll get it."

Well, I knew I wasn't any kind of fisherman, so I could not rely on my own skills anyway. I sat down and took a deep breath in of God confidence and waited. About 20-30 minutes later, I got what I thought was a snag on my line, but it turned out definitely to be a fish!

My husband began to coach me, and then the captain came to do the same. He told me, as I was reeling the big fish in, that I probably had a giant snapper on the end of my line. I was so surprised that he knew what it was before the fish became visible! Sure enough, as I continued to reel and pull, my 20-pound giant red snapper surfaced!

I was thanking God with so much joy and excitement. I knew I had had a breakthrough in my belief system. I just kept remembering your stories of confidence and thought that I was capable of the same faith and be-lief. I persevered through, and it paid off.

> *Thank you for your ministry and for writing the books, including Faith Hunt. I am grateful and thankful to God and to your ministry that have helped me move into greater blessings. I look forward to the future with even more faith and excitement. I know how much this experience also ministered to our family!*
>
> —S.T.

YOUR FAITH HUNT

Today's date: _____ Time: _____

Today, I prayed the prayer of faith for:

_____

_____

_____

_____

_____

_____

_____

Date of answered prayer: _____

My Faith Hunt story:

_____

_____

_____

_____

_____

_____

_____

_____

DAY 17
YOU HAVE A LEGAL AGREEMENT

He remembers his covenant forever, the promise he made, for a thousand generations, the covenant he made with Abraham, the oath he swore to Isaac. He confirmed it to Jacob as a decree, to Israel as an everlasting covenant.

—Psalm 105:8-10

Covenant—a legal agreement between two or more parties that brings a relationship of commitment; a contract.

As a believer, you have a covenant with God, and the blessing of the Lord—the covenant of God—legally supersedes the earth curse system.

How? It started with Abraham. Abraham made a covenant with God. That legal agreement gave heaven an open door into the earth realm. Then, Abraham had children and grandchildren. Jesus Christ was in that lineage. That's why the first book in the New Testament—Matthew—starts with a genealogy, because in the earth realm, it proved to Satan that Jesus was *legally* an heir of Abraham and could legally walk into the earth realm.

Abraham's faith and the covenant that followed gave God legal access to Abraham and his heirs—believers, you.

Deuteronomy 28 lists the blessings of the Lord—the promises. Those are your legal rights, how your life should look, your legal destiny, and your inheritance as a child of God. Those aren't just Old Testament promises. Galatians 3:14 says, "He redeemed us in order that the blessing given to Abraham might come to the Gentiles through Jesus Christ." Paul goes on and says, "So that by faith we might receive the promise of the Spirit of God."

Remember Joseph? He had the promises *in prison*—a completely hopeless situation—and he still prospered. He was still promoted in prison! Of course, he was successful when Potiphar put him in charge of all of Egypt. Joseph was successful in *everything* he puts his hands to. It didn't matter that Egypt was in a famine for seven years—a famine that affected the *entire* Middle East. The Bible tells us that Joseph had stored up huge quantities of grain like the sand of the sea. It was so much that he stopped keeping a record!

Stop for a minute and really get that picture in your mind: a grain pile so enormous that it couldn't be contained, let alone counted.

That's the picture you should have in your mind of the promises of God in your life—a grain pile so enormous that it can't be contained!

Here's the thing: the Bible says you have *even more* promises because you've been restored back to God and have the Spirit of God living *inside* of you (Hebrews 8:6).

You have an even greater advantage than Joseph! God is with you. You should be prospering. You should have success in *everything* you do.

> "What you have is yours legally; but once you give it to God, then and only then can he get involved with the seed and multiply it back to you. It gives Him access to move on your behalf."
> —Gary Keesee

"This gun is amazing!" I said, astounded as another Sabat slug found its mark within inches of the previous rounds.

"You like it? It's the best gun for Ohio hunting," my dad smiled proudly. It was a Savage Slug gun with mossy oak camo finish. A Keesee family tradition was to get a gun for my birthday as the event fell right at gun season's full swing.

"Like it? I love it!" I smiled back. "I almost feel like this gun makes it too easy... maybe I should believe God

for a headshot," I joked. My dad looked at me with an all too familiar look. It was the same look he gave me when I told him that I was considering spear hunting wild boar or that I chased a pack of coyotes with a sword. I hunt for different reasons than just simply to have meat (that part is a benefit). I like to challenge myself; marksmanship is a self-defining sport. Your skill is defined by simple terms: you hit or miss.

"You aren't going to do that," my dad said, almost reading my thoughts.

"I might," I said back with a sheepish grin. "What if I believe God for a headshot?"

"Why would you do that?"

"I want to challenge myself. Besides, the meat will stay intact and the animal feels no pain," I made my case.

"I guess if that's what you want to do and believe for, God can give you that opportunity," my dad said with a shake of his head.

I questioned if this was something that I should do. I didn't ever want to risk injuring a deer or causing them a cruel end. My father had always taught us to respect God's creations and that deer were there for *our enjoyment, but we had to steward the earth.*

As I pondered it with my head, my spirit responded, "I am the God of the impossible. I am up for the challenge if you are."

I determined in that moment that I would indeed believe God for more than just a simple hunt that could easily be written off as a coincidence. I would believe Him for a testimony.

That night I sowed my seed and believed God, as I did every year, but this time the check read, "buck, headshot." I knew that, according to Mark 11:24, I believed that I received when I prayed, and my spirit leapt with excitement. As I planted my harvest, I whispered under my breath, "All right, God, let's do this."

The next morning was brisk and dark as Ohio mornings have a tendency of being. I peered out the window at the distant treeline that shrouded the horizon. In those dark woods, I would face my hardest shot yet, because I asked for it. I headed downstairs to the smell of eggs and cheese with sausage—a nostalgic pre-hunt breakfast that has been a tradition for as long as I can remember. My brother soon joined us in the kitchen and sat down to eat.

"That gun is almost cheating," he said as we talked about the day ahead.

"That's why I'm just going to believe for a headshot."

He looked at me with disbelief. "I guess that's one way to do it."

"I'm serious," I affirmed.

My dad glanced out the window as a thin strip of purple and gold peeked over the treetops. "We had better get going," he said.

We layered up and headed out for what was sure to be an exciting hunt. The air was sharp as it reached for my breath. The Savage hung over my right shoulder as I followed in stride behind my father and brother. We crossed the open field and headed for the woods but not without stopping at the edge of the field to pray.

"All right, boys, we know what the Word of God says. Today, we are receiving our deer," my father said. He then proceeded to pray over our hunt and for safety. "Amen," we agreed in unity.

"I will see you guys after I get my headshot," I said as I headed down the lane and toward my neck of

the woods. I had always hunted the same section of the woods. It had become a place of rest for me, like returning to your old bedroom after being gone at college.

I unslung my new gun from my right shoulder and now held it in both hands, scanning the dark mist ahead of me as I neared the woods. The winds began to pick up as I neared the forest's edge. The sun peeked through the treetops, fighting to light my path as I made my way further into the woods. I scanned the area as I made my way to the tree. I had been here before. Many times, I had made the climb and waited for my harvest. But today, this would be different.

The woods were silent, save the whistle of wind through the gently rocking trees. I made my way to the top, checked my scope, and made sure I had a round chambered before settling in. I was rocking about 35 feet from the ground, facing the way I had entered the woods. Almost instantly, I heard the distant sound of leaves crunching underfoot. I went through my mental checklist. Don't move suddenly, check for visual confirmation, and be prepared for frustration when it turns out to be a squirrel.

I turned my head ever so slowly to the right as the distant sound became louder and more consistent. I quickly realized this was no squirrel. This was a buck, and he was making his way straight toward me. I pulled the gun up preemptively and waited to get my eyes on him. He came in from my right at a sprint, zigzagging through the trees like a professional skier. My instincts kicked in as I adjusted the zoom on my scope to the lowest setting and pulled up for a running shot. I had him in my sight, leading him as he ran. At this point, he made a hard right turn and went behind some brush. My finger became heavy on the trigger. I knew he would clear the brush broadside and I would have a clean shot available. I focused as the deer crossed my sight line, taking in a breath slowly to steady my aim... and nothing. It wasn't that the deer had changed his path. It was that I had remembered mine.

As the 6-point ran through my crosshairs, the Holy Spirit reminded me of what I had asked for, a head-shot. As much as I would have liked to take a shot at a deer at a full run through the trees and think that I could hit him in the head, I knew I didn't have the cowboy in me to take the shot. I lowered the gun and watched the deer run over the edge of a small embankment and out of sight. I sat there for a second thinking to myself, Did you really just let that deer go? Then all at once, I felt peace and faith rise up within me. I said, "In the name of Jesus, deer, you will come back and give me a perfect shot at your head."

Everything in me was thinking, I have really lost it. This is the dumbest thing any hunter has done save shooting themselves in the foot. Maybe I just did in a manner of speaking. But I knew my mind wasn't in control; my spirit was the driving force. The Word of God was clear, and God wasn't a man that He should lie. This was going to manifest in the natural because I knew it already had in my spirit.

I readied my gun, pulling it into my shoulder and watching the ridgeline. Ten minutes... still no deer. It felt as though an eternity passed as I waited for what I knew was coming... the headshot. I could hear my heart beat as I saw antlers eclipse the ridge.

Slowly, the buck walked back toward me. I almost laughed out loud with excitement. He kept coming in, his whole body visible now as he made a line directly toward me. I pulled up slowly as the wind picked up in violent gales. This was my moment. Click! The safety went off under the weight of my thumb as I looked down through the scope. Just as the buck came into range for my new weapon, he did something that surprised me. He stopped and laid down behind a log 120 yards away and turned his head so that all that was visible was the back of it. You have got to be kidding me!!! I thought to myself. There was literally no other shot to take but a headshot! Could the Kingdom of God really be THAT specific?

I slowly slid out of the chair of my stand and took a knee, desperately trying to steady myself in the violent gusts of wind. My heart was pounding at this point. Here I was about to take a 120-yard shot at the back of a deer's head in the middle of a windstorm. I knew I couldn't miss. This was a one-time shot.

Left and right the trees swayed. Rather than correct, I simply timed my rhythm with the trees. My heart slowed and I honed in. All at once, the gun lurched as I fired off a round, nearly falling out of the tree. As the smoke cleared, I couldn't see the deer. I climbed down as quickly as I could manage without jumping and made my way toward the fallen tree. To my amazement, there was the deer laying facedown. I had made the shot! I shouted for joy and left with a story to tell. God's Kingdom is THAT specific, and faith works every time!

The look on my dad's face was priceless when I returned with a beaming smile. I answered as if reading his thoughts, "I got my headshot."

He smiled knowingly. "Let's go get 'em."

—Tom Keesee

YOUR FAITH HUNT

Today's date: _____ Time: _____

Today, I prayed the prayer of faith for:

_____

_____

_____

_____

_____

_____

_____

_____

Date of answered prayer: _____

My Faith Hunt story:

_____

_____

_____

_____

_____

_____

_____

_____

DAY 18

REFUSE TO SETTLE OR
BACK DOWN

The weapons we fight with are not the weapons of the world. On the contrary, they have divine power to demolish strongholds. We demolish arguments and every pretension that sets itself up against the knowledge of God, and we take captive every thought to make it obedient to Christ.

—2 Corinthians 10:4-5

What's holding you back?

What's keeping you from doing what you want to do in life?

What's keeping you from doing what God has called you to do?

If you're like most people, you have at least one reason. Maybe you think you're too young, or you're too old, that you don't have enough experience, or enough of the "right" kind of experience, that you don't have enough money, or you've made too many mistakes. Maybe your past is what's holding you back.

I've been there.

Throughout my life, I've had all sorts of reasons not to move forward with the things God was calling me to do. In fact, at one time or another, I've probably told myself every one of the reasons I just gave you.

But most of those reasons were really just excuses I was giving myself because I was afraid.

Don't give up on God's plan just because you're afraid, or because you face obstacles or hurdles.

You have to refuse to settle, to quit, or to back down.

Of course, we sometimes need to be patient with our aspirations, but most of the time, our problem isn't that we're trying to move things ahead too quickly but that, at some point, we adapted to cope with negative situations in life and then we parked there.

It's easy to get stuck in a rut.

Is that you? Are behaviors, habits, and old patterns of thinking and acting holding you back from being the best you can be and living the life God wants for you?

That's called a stronghold—something you've believed for so long that it becomes truth in your life. It becomes the truth even if it's really a lie.

And if you allow yourself to believe a lie, it might as well be the truth.

Because if you believe that you're ugly, you're going to act like you're ugly. If you believe you can't do something, you're probably not even going to try to do it. If you believe no one will ever love you, then you're not going to project anything lovable to anyone.

The good news is that you can overthrow and destroy strongholds. God didn't purpose you for a life of failure. The key to walking in your full potential is to tap into the amazing ability to see life from God's perspective. You can say, "Now wait a minute. I used to believe this, but this is not what the Word of God says about me or my life."

It may be tough, but you can do it. Remember Philippians 4:13 (NKJV) says, "I can do all things through Christ who strengthens me."

So, take a step forward. Measure what you say and believe against what God's Word says in order to know what is really the truth. Take thoughts captive that don't line up with what the Bible says and cast them down.

It doesn't matter how long you've had the stronghold in your life; you have the power to overcome through Jesus.

> "God has called and equipped you to be a conqueror. You weren't made to back down, or run, or hide; you were made to engage the problem and be victorious. Your dream is on the other side of the battle."
>
> —Gary Keesee

Recently, I listened to the original "Your Financial Revolution" messages when you were talking about Peter's great catch of fish and how "it would be easy to catch the fish if Jesus tells you where they are." That phrase jumped out at me every time I listened to that message, and I had been thinking about it for a couple of weeks.

One day I had a vision of fishing in a pond on my grandmother's farm. It's a pond I have fished in for largemouth bass off and on for most of my life and have caught dozens of them on red shad plastic worms. When I saw this glimpse, I saw where I was standing, which direction I was casting, and even the YELLOW SPINNER BAIT I was using. I knew we were going there in a couple of weeks to celebrate my grandmother's 90th birthday.

The morning we were getting ready, I was putting my boys and my fishing gear in the truck and opened my tackle box to look for yellow spinner bait. I didn't have one. I have my dad's old tackle box in the garage, so I looked there. The yellow spinner bait was there. I grabbed it and headed to the farm.

We had our birthday time and some cake and coffee, and I told the boys it was time to fish. Up until this time none of us—cousins, brothers, or in-laws—could remember anything over three or four pounds being caught there. I boldly said, "There are big bass in that pond. I know it."

We got there, I got the boys rigged up, and I tied on my yellow spinner bait. I went to the spot I thought I saw in my vision, but it didn't seem exactly right. After two or three casts, I realized I needed to move around

the pond. I walked to another spot and realized that was it. On about the third cast, my spinner bait looped over a branch, I dangled it in and out of the water a few times and then flipped it back over the branch and into the pond.

Almost immediately, it took off like a shot. I set the hook and realized this was no four-pounder. As I reeled her in, I called for someone to come and take my picture. After I landed her, my nephew, an avid angler, and I estimated her weight at seven to eight pounds!

What a joy to be able to share that experience with my sons and other family members! As we rode home, I was able to share with my wife and boys how faithful God is to show us things and to bring blessings beyond what we could ever ask or think!

—Asher C.

YOUR FAITH HUNT

Today's date: _____ Time: _____

Today, I prayed the prayer of faith for:

_____

_____

_____

_____

_____

_____

_____

Date of answered prayer: _____

My Faith Hunt story:

_____

_____

_____

_____

_____

_____

_____

_____

_____

DAY 19
GET THE RIGHT PICTURE

For as he thinks in his heart, so is he.

—Proverbs 23:7 (NKJV)

Have you ever bought a seed packet? You know, the ones from the lawn and garden stores?

If you have, you probably didn't just choose one based on the name, right?

No, what you probably noticed was the *picture* on the front.

If you bought flower seeds, the picture on the front was probably of big, beautiful, brightly colored, flourishing flowers. If you bought fruit or vegetable seeds, the picture on the front was probably of an oversized, lush-looking version of that fruit or vegetable.

Why do they put pictures like that on seed packets? Because we all know that seeing a picture of a tiny little sprout or a shriveled up seed on the front of those packets wouldn't motivate us to buy those seeds; neither would a picture of a person working in their garden covered in dirt and wiping beads of sweat from his or her forehead.

The pictures on the outside of those packets motivate us to produce the end result.

It's the same way with your thoughts.

Your thoughts are like the pictures on the outside of those seed packets.

What you listen to, what you look at, the things you do, and the friends you hang around all produce thoughts—*pictures*—in your mind whether you realize it or not. When you begin to concentrate on those pictures, those thoughts produce a desire for the end result, for good or for bad.

In fact, the Bible says that desire *drags* us. It produces a plan to get what it wants, and that plan can take you to a place you never thought you'd be. Don't get me wrong—that can be a good thing if you're thinking about good things, like the promises of God, or an amazing garden full of fruits and vegetables that look just like those seed packet pictures. Your good desires can help guide you toward success.

The problem is that your heart can't tell the difference between a good picture/thought/desire or an evil picture/thought/desire. That's where you have to get a handle on things, because this is nothing to play with.

It's life and death.

Because if you have the wrong pictures—you're constantly thinking negative or wrong thoughts—there's no way you're moving forward toward what God has for you.

At best, you're probably stagnant or slightly off course. At worst, you're heading in the opposite direction of the destination God has for you.

I know because I've been there; I spent years thinking destructive thoughts of fear, discontentment, and failure. Those thoughts kept me in a downward spiral.

I was a believer, but my thoughts were a disaster.

Drenda and I began to learn how the Kingdom of God operates, and it was like someone flipped a light switch. We started changing our thoughts, our *pictures*.

You have the same authority.

Second Corinthians 10:5 says that we're to take captive every thought to make it obedient to Christ. Plain and simple, your brain does not have the authority to think anything it wants.

You can *choose* what you think about.

Philippians 4:8 instructs us: "Whatever is noble, whatever is right, whatever is pure, whatever is lovely, whatever is admirable—if anything is excellent or praiseworthy—think about such things."

It's so critical that you really get this, for your faith hunt and for your future.

You can choose what you think about! You don't have to think on everything that pops into your head. You can choose your thoughts. You can choose your pictures.

"When you analyze what happens in stories of real change in people's lives, you'll almost always find the same scenarios—they made the decision to change their thoughts."

—Gary Keesee

I love hunting—a lot. I have been hunting since I was 11 years old, and have had many memorable hunts in the last nine years. Several years ago, my dad purchased your book Faith Hunt. As an avid hunter and a Christian, I read it. One, because who doesn't love reading about hunting? And two, I was interested in seeing how applying the biblical principles of sowing and reaping could work in hunting.

As I read more of the book, I began to understand that God loves to bless His children, not just in the financial world, or with signs and wonders, but in every aspect of our lives. Gary's stories, not just about hunting but of fishing and sowing seeds for other people, inspired me to try it myself.

Fast forward to my 18th birthday. My family has a tradition of going to eastern Montana every fall to hunt during the mule deer rut, and this year was no exception. My mom and sister couldn't make the trip this year, so it was just going to be my dad and me. We loaded up the truck and headed east on the six-hour road trip. As we were driving, we were discussing previous hunts and how Gary talked in his book about sowing and reaping, and how many times we had seen God's hand in our hunting trips since we had read his book years before.

We decided to put this hunt into God's hands and to believe for two bucks, one for each of us. I prayed for a buck larger than any other buck I had ever seen before, and one with at least one kicker point or extra trash on the horns—a non-typical buck. Dad decided to pray and believe for a buck with a drop tine.

We arrived at our camp and laid out a game plan of where to hunt and how many days we were going to be there. With four days of good weather before a snowstorm was forecasted to hit, we decided on a new area we had never been to, and to go for a hike into a burned-out forest area to see what we could find.

We saw nothing that first evening, so we prayed that night and asked the Lord where we should go the next day. We both prayed and felt like we were supposed to go to another area a few miles down the road. But all that next day, we didn't see a single buck.

With thoughts of doubt and discouragement starting to creep in, we prayed for clarity and wisdom. I told dad I believed that we should go to a place we had gone to a few years ago and had had some success. We packed up the truck and headed back toward town a ways then pulled off onto another forest service road. We slept that night in the car and got up bright and early, hoping to be alone and away from the weekend warriors. We headed up an old logging road, and as the sun came up, we started seeing deer and quickly spotted a very nice buck. As we studied it, we came to the realization that this buck was bigger than any other deer we had ever seen. Could this be the one?

However, as we watched him chasing does, we determined that he did not have any extra points; he was just a very nice typical buck. So, I decided, although I would have been very happy to take him, that he was not my buck.

About this time, we heard another vehicle approaching and quickly realized it was coming up the old road behind us, would come very close to these deer, and could spook them. I ran back to the road just in time to catch the truck, and I told them about the deer up ahead. They quickly jumped out, and I led them back to where we had last seen the buck. They asked why I didn't want to shoot it, and I told them that I was praying for something bigger and that I was believing that God had a better buck for me.

We said good-bye to them and good luck, and Dad and I backed up and went around them, hoping they succeeded in shooting that buck. As we continued hiking, I couldn't help but wonder if I had made a mistake passing up a buck like that one. But I was still believing for my buck, so we kept hiking.

An hour or so later, we spotted more deer in a draw, bedded down in the shade of the afternoon. We thought there was another good looking buck in the group, so we snuck into rifle range just to see. Sure enough, there was a good looking buck there! We waited for 15 minutes or so, and when he turned his head, we saw, yep, this one had some extra points! That was my buck.

We snuck even closer, until we were about 190 yards away or so. I laid down and got a steady rest, calmed down, and Dad was watching through his binoculars.

I squeezed off my shot. The buck just rolled over in his bed, never even getting up.

My dad and I high-fived, thanked God for another amazing hunt, and headed down to put my hands on my buck. It was an amazing hunt, and God showed up yet again!

—Josiah T.

YOUR FAITH HUNT

Today's date: _____ Time: _____

Today, I prayed the prayer of faith for:

_____

_____

_____

_____

_____

_____

_____

Date of answered prayer: _____

My Faith Hunt story:

_____

_____

_____

_____

_____

_____

_____

_____

DAY 20
UNCOVER THE
TREASURE

"I am the Lord, the God of all mankind. Is anything too hard for me?"
—Jeremiah 32:27

One of my favorite stories in the Bible is in Daniel 2.

We read that King Nebuchadnezzar had some disturbing dreams that really upset him, and he couldn't sleep. When he called in his magicians, enchanters, sorcerers, and astrologers, they expected him to tell them the dream so they could interpret it. But King Nebuchadnezzar threw them all a curveball and told them they needed to tell him *what* he had dreamed *and* the interpretation. And, if they didn't, he would have them "cut into pieces and their houses turned into piles of rubble."

How's that for an impossible demand? I mean, really. Can you imagine someone saying, "Tell me what I dreamed and what it means or I'll have you killed"? Clearly, King Nebuchadnezzar wasn't rational. The guy wasn't getting any sleep, after all. When the guys couldn't do what he demanded, he ordered the execution of all the wise men of Babylon—which included Daniel and his friends.

Daniel asked for more time. Then, he went to his friends and told them to pray so they wouldn't be killed.

Daniel wasn't just in a hard spot. He was facing a death sentence!

But Daniel knew there is nothing that is hidden from God; he knew *nothing is too hard for God.*

Daniel 2:19 tells us that the mystery was revealed to Daniel during the night. In verses 20-23, Daniel praised God. Then he went to the king and asked that he not execute anyone. Daniel revealed the dream and interpreted it, and King Nebuchadnezzar honored Daniel and promoted him.

Stop here for a second. Because I need you to realize that this isn't just a great Bible story—*this applies to YOUR life.*

See, Jesus made our access to the Kingdom legal, yet most people read the stories in the Bible much like our ancestors viewed things like electricity and lightning—acknowledging that, yes, the events happened but never envisioning the POWER of those things for themselves.

You may not be facing a death sentence like Daniel was, but you still need powerful answers from God; you need Him to direct your steps in your faith hunt, and in your life.

That's your victory—your secret weapon. Jesus said that the same things that we see Him doing, we have the ability to do as well. The Kingdom of God has already been given to YOU. You just have to understand its laws. Because it's the Kingdom *in you* that gives you access to the secret knowledge—the hidden knowledge.

It's like a hidden treasure that's out there waiting for you. You just need a Word of Knowledge from God to uncover it. You just need something you didn't know before to be revealed to you, so you can move on it and do whatever it takes to capture it.

"You have these rights and benefits as a believer. Are they sitting out there unclaimed? Are you missing out?"

—Gary Keesee

I've always wanted to shoot an 8-point buck or bigger for my first one. Year after year I sowed my seed, hoping I would get my buck, but I never did. In fact, when I went out, I often found myself cold and ready to get out of the tree after half an hour. I knew I was just going through the motions.

Hope is the counterfeit of faith. It sounds the same—it can even look the same—but it doesn't produce the same results. I always hoped I would get my buck every year—I didn't know.

This year, I knew that I knew that I was going to get my buck. I sowed my seed on October 28th, and my husband and I went hunting that night at my parents' property. A buck showed up, but I didn't see him until he was too close and I couldn't get my bow up for a shot without him seeing me. I missed my opportunity, but I wasn't discouraged because he had shown up. I knew if he had shown up once, I could get him to show up again.

My dad has taught me that when your deer shows up and you make a mistake, you need to re-sow your seed, so that's exactly what I did. I sowed my seed again the next day, and my husband and I went out again. I knew I wasn't leaving that tree without my buck showing up. I was out for about 45 minutes when I prayed, "Okay, God, send him my way now. I'm getting uncomfortable in this stand." Ha! The tree I was sitting in looked out over the woods and opened up to a soybean field about 100 yards away. Just then, I saw a tail twitch through the bushes out in that field far to the left. That was all I could see, but I knew that was my deer.

I used my grunt call, and the deer came trotting to-ward me into the woods. I could see it was a buck, but I couldn't tell how big it was at that distance. I wasn't going to wait until he was close enough to find out.

This time, I was determined to get my shot. I got my bow into place as he crossed through the trees. The adrenaline was indescribable—heart racing, hands shaking, struggling to keep my bow steady because I was breathing so hard.

When he came into a clearing 50 yards from my tree, I took my shot!

The next few minutes were a chaotic blur. The buck took off running, some deer kicked up to my right, and I sat there in shock. I didn't even think to look at the trail the buck ran down! It was the first time I had ever shot my bow at a buck—in fact, it was the first time I had shot my bow this year!

Once my heart stopped pounding, I got down and began looking for some kind of evidence that I had hit the deer, because I really had no idea if it was a good shot. I couldn't find any blood, fur, or my arrow. I whispered, "Okay, Holy Spirit, help me find this arrow."

I walked around for a few more minutes when my foot caught on a bush. I looked down, and in between my boots was the arrow! It had somehow broken, and the fletching (neon feathers) on the arrow were gone, which made it virtually impossible to see in the brush at dusk. The arrow had blood and fur on both ends, so I knew the arrow had cleared both sides of the deer. That was a good sign!

I looked for blood around the area I found the arrow, but I couldn't find one drop. As darkness settled in, my husband joined me from his tree, and we both began looking for a blood trail.

"Where did he run?" my husband asked.

"Well, it was somewhere that way..." I said, pointing to the vast woods.

"You didn't pay attention to which path he ran down?" my husband said, laughing.

"It was all a blur! The adrenaline was so crazy, I just kind of blacked out in the moment."

"Well, where exactly was he standing when you shot him?"

"Well... those yellow leaves over there were in my scope when I shot, so maybe up by that bush, or right here, or somewhere back there...."

My husband looked at me with a disbelieving smile.

"How big was he?" he asked.

"I don't know!" I laughed.

We searched the whole area and couldn't find one speck of blood. I prayed under my breath again, "Holy Spirit, lead us to this deer."

My phone died (which I was using as my flashlight), so we decided we would walk up to the house to get my dad's large flashlights. We called him and told him the news and asked where we could find them. During our conversation, my dad mentioned the shot might be a gut shot or a flesh wound since there wasn't any blood, which wasn't ideal. A gut shot could mean the deer wouldn't die for hours and could travel far. A flesh wound could mean the deer wouldn't die at all.

"Deer always go downhill when they're hurt," my dad said.

I told my husband, Elijah, "While we're walking back, let's just follow the general direction I saw him go and see if we find any blood. It goes downhill over there." Even though we couldn't find any blood, I still felt completely confident that I had my buck.

We began walking back in the dark with one flash-

light, eventually wandering off of the trail and into the dry creek bed in my parents' woods back toward their house. It was the fastest route. We were at least 500 yards away from where I shot the deer when my husband exclaimed, "Blood!" There were three small specks of blood on a leaf in the middle of the creek bed—and, miraculously, my husband saw it!

We spotted the tiny blood trail and slowly started following it. It wasn't easy. There wasn't much blood, and it was small and far and few in between. We tracked the blood trail for about 10 yards, when suddenly we heard a deer jump up somewhere in front of us and run. We heard it travel a short distance and then get quiet again.

"That has to be him!" my husband said. "We don't want him to keep traveling, so let's mark this spot and come back in a few hours or in the morning." He took off a blue jacket he had under his camo and tied it to a tree.

My dad said we should wait until the morning because it seemed like a gut shot with so little blood, and those can take hours upon hours for the deer to die. I didn't want my deer to die a slow and painful death! I prayed that he would die quickly right where we heard him stop, and it would be peaceful for him.

My dad, Elijah, and I went out at 5:30 a.m. the next morning. We started tracking the blood trail again, but the further we went, the less blood there was. The drops were tiny and far apart.

"It's really weird there isn't more blood. It's not looking too good," my dad said as we all searched for the next clue with no success. His comment went in one ear and out the other—I felt completely confident my deer was going to be waiting for me a few yards ahead where we heard him stop.

Suddenly, the blood trail was gone. We couldn't find a drip anywhere. We had only tracked about 50 yards total from the place we saw the first blood drop when my husband, who had walked a short distance ahead, yelled out, "Here he is!"

"You found blood?" I yelled back.

"No, the deer! He's right here!" my husband exclaimed, running over to the buck and shining his flashlight on him. "You did it! You got him!"

My dad and I were quick on his heels in amazement. For the first time I got to see how big he was, and he was a perfect 8-pointer. I was ecstatic! We discovered I had shot him through the heart and lungs. He had died exactly where we heard him stop the night before within a few minutes of us being there, just like I prayed! My dad and I were even more excited because we were working on this book (Your Faith Hunt), and it was only a few days before it was going to print! God's timing is awesome!

—Kirsten (Keesee) McKinney

YOUR FAITH HUNT
A 21-day Devotional and Prayer Journal

YOUR FAITH HUNT

Today's date: _____ Time: _____

Today, I prayed the prayer of faith for:

_____

_____

_____

_____

_____

_____

_____

_____

Date of answered prayer: _____

My Faith Hunt story:

_____

_____

_____

_____

_____

_____

_____

_____

_____

DAY 21
SHARE THE STORIES

Come and hear, all you who fear God; let me tell you what he has done for me.

—Psalm 66:16

Did you know that there is a Faith Hall of Fame?

It isn't a really cool building with trophies or pictures or busts of Abraham and Moses or anything, but it is recorded in the Bible.

Hebrews 11 is the Faith Hall of Fame. It's the story of the heritage of the children of God. It's a record of the mighty things that ordinary people did with God.

You should have a story like Hebrews 11 for *your* life. Because people are looking at your life, and they're reading your story.

So, what's your story?

What do people see when they look at you?

What do they see about God when they look at your life?

Does your life look any different than the rest of the world's? Are you demonstrating God's love and His Kingdom to a world that is watching you?

I know. Life can be tough, and your flesh would like to just sit around and drink lemonade. It doesn't want to deal with pressure. It wants to escape. It wants smooth sailing. But you'll never be happy doing that all of the time.

And, quite frankly, lemonade and smooth sailing don't make for very interesting stories.

No, the best stories are about the journeys, the tribulations and the pressures, and how they were overcome.

That's what God wants for your life. He created you for a special and specific assignment. He wants you to have great stories.

See, Mark 16:15 tells us to go into the world and share the Good News of the Gospel, but we misinterpret the term "good news." John 3:16 tells us how much God loves people and how important people are to Him, but in case you haven't noticed, John 3:16 isn't good news to the world. It doesn't mean a thing to them.

The world is looking for the *stories*, the ones that say they can have happy marriages and strong families; the ones that say they can have their bills paid and their houses paid off; the stories of faith hunts so incredible that they can only be possible because of God.

When John the Baptist wanted to be sure that Jesus was the promised Messiah, he sent a few of his disciples to find out if Jesus was the one. When they asked Jesus if He was the one to come, He didn't start quoting Isaiah or Jeremiah, or any of the many prophecies about Him to prove He was the one. No, He said, "Tell John what you have seen—the blind eyes are opened, people are healed, lepers are cleansed, and good news has been preached to the poor."

Jesus was basically saying, "Go back and tell John what you saw. Go back and tell John the *stories* of the Kingdom and the people's lives that were changed."

People want to see the results of the Kingdom. They like to hear good news. They want to know that there is hope for them and for their situation. The problem is there are too many Christians who don't have much good news to share. They have religion, but they don't have much good news. And the devil loves that, because no one wants to serve a God like that.

It's the stories that bring evidence that the Kingdom is real and *here*.

Just like the stories placed throughout this book give you hope for your own faith hunts, your stories will give others hope. So go... share your stories of what God has done.

"You can be around people all of the time, but if you're not careful, you will never actually see them. But God sees them, and He knows everything about them. And He needs your help to reach them."

—Gary Keesee

As a long time hunter, I've learned how to scout deer, track their patterns, and systematically go after what I want. It's my hobby, I love it, and I've been quite successful at it. This year, I wasn't seeing any promising deer in my typical pre-season scouting.

Late in July, I happened to be fishing at a private pond where I spotted a very promising buck grazing in the field. This was my buck! This was the one I was going after. The only problem I could identify was that this buck was several miles from any of my hunting spots. I quickly found out from other hunters that no one else was hunting this particular spot. Encouraged, I set out to talk with the land owner to inquire about getting permission, and it was quickly granted. I sowed my seed to harvest this buck, and I had written permission to hunt the land.

Over the next several months, I planned and prepared by investing my time and money. I visited the property daily, set up trail cameras, and purchased and installed a new tree stand. It was a lot of work, but all of my experience had taught me that this would pay off. I was going to be in the right place at the right time, and I would harvest this deer. I had it all planned out.

After several months of my routine, I received a call from a fellow hunter who had become an acquaintance. This was not a friendly call. Contrary to what I had been told, there had been someone hunting in my new spot, and it was him. Unbeknownst to me, he had been hunting this very location for several years. In my excitement, I did not see his flattened blind hidden in the summer foliage a mere 20 yards from where I put my stand. All season, day in and day out, I saw no signs of anyone visiting this location. Nevertheless, he was adamant that I had to go. I made the argument that I truly did not know he was there and I had put so much of myself into this location. My efforts to work out a plan for us to share the spot were not welcomed. The land owner, wishing to avoid conflict, asked if we could work it out, but my acquaintance did not budge. This was his spot. After a few days, the land owner kindly rescinded my permission.

I was crushed, misunderstood, and defeated. All of my diligence was stripped away, and someone else was going to reap the reward for which I had sown. It didn't take much time for bitterness to set in. I spent a few days wallowing in my own pity. Knowing my heart wasn't right and understanding there are two sides to every story, I knew what I needed to do. I made a call to the acquaintance. Perhaps I called at a bad time or perhaps he avoided my call, but what happened next was crucial. I left him a heartfelt message wishing him luck this season and apologizing for any problems I caused. While I never heard back, that didn't matter. I did what I had to do. I forgave him.

Not long after, that still, small voice reminded me of something. On July 29th, I had sown for that very deer. It wasn't contingent on location or a specific timeline or how I had pictured it in my mind at the time. That buck was mine, and I shifted my thinking. For the next few months, I was resolute. At times, in the natural, I thought there was no way that deer would come to me. But God is bigger than our "no way" thinking.

After two months of having no sight of my buck, he came to my old spot. I wasn't there the first time but got a picture of him. The next night, I was in my stand, confident and expectant. He would come to me. It wasn't long before I heard the rustling of the leaves and got sight of him approaching my stand. He was bigger than I remembered! That buck walked right in to me, within shooting range. As I pulled back my bow, I startled a doe and he was about to take off too. I was able to get a perfect shot, and he dropped within 40 yards! Immediately, I thanked Jesus! His promises are real. No matter the circumstance or people that come our way, his Word prevails. To make it even better, I got word that my acquaintance harvested a monster buck as well, a few days before I got mine. God's blessings are abundant. He has more than enough for all of us.

—Dustin M.